THE MINISTRY OF STATE FOR URBAN AFFAIRS

A COURAGEOUS EXPERIMENT IN PUBLIC ADMINISTRATION

1987
The Centre for Human Settlements
Faculty of Graduate Studies
The University of British Columbia
Vancouver, Canada

THE MINISTRY OF STATE FOR URBAN AFFAIRS:
A COURAGEOUS EXPERIMENT IN PUBLIC ADMINISTRATION

Canadian Cataloguing in Publication Data

Main entry under title:

The Ministry of State for Urban Affairs: a courageous
    experiment in public administration

    1. Canada. Urban Affairs Canada—History. 2.
Urban policy—Canada—History. I. Oberlander,
H. Peter, 1922- II. Fallick, Arthur Laurence,
1955- III. University of British Columbia.
Centre for Human Settlements.

JL103.U72M55 1987   354.71'06818   C88-091054-2

ISBN-0-88865-331-X
Printed in Canada
Price $12.

TABLE OF CONTENTS

iv

SECTION THREE—Assessment and Review

SECTION FOUR—Future Need

INTRODUCTION

For a number of years the UBC Centre for Human Settlements has had on its agenda a concern about documenting the story of the Ministry of State for Urban Affairs. The opportunity and the impetus came as a result of a major program on the federal role in urban affairs, convened during the Canadian Urban Studies Conference, August 14-17, 1985 by the Institute of Urban Studies at the University of Winnipeg. Under the chairmanship of Professor Brahm Wiesman, Director of the School of Community and Regional Planning at the the University of British Columbia, this program brought together a number of academics and professionals who actively participated in the creation and management of the Ministry of State for Urban Affairs in Ottawa in the early 70s. Senator Michael Pitfield led the presentation with his paper on 'The Origins of the Ministry of State for Urban Affairs', followed by presentations on 'Research Based Urban Policy', 'The Rationalization of Federal Urban Programs' and 'The Ministry and the Intergovernmental Dimension of Urban Affairs'. This initiative of the Institute of Urban Studies, University of Winnipeg, provided a beginning of collecting papers from a number of active participants in the early stages of the Ministry and allowed them to reflect on their own particular role during those critical years. The papers presented at the Canadian Urban Studies Programme in Winnipeg have been augmented by several other presentations and represent a contribution to the growing literature on federal institution building particularly in urban affairs. There is no attempt made at comprehensiveness nor are the papers and their presentation in this volume meant to be a definitive analysis of the Ministry's role and performance. Indeed the papers are written and presented by those involved in the process of initiating and running the Ministry, they are not written from a detached or absolutely objective perspective. The authors were intimately involved in the ebb and flow of launching an experiment in public administration, and have the scars to prove their personal role and participation. It is not a detached, academic presentation, it is a presentation of what happened, warts and all, by those who made it happen.

One of the participants at the Winnipeg Seminar was John Sewell who played a critical role on Toronto City Council and subsequently as Mayor of Toronto. Subsequent to the Conference, John Sewell wrote a column in the Globe and Mail on August 20, 1985 headed 'A Ministry Remembered':

> . . . The ministry—everyone refers to it as MSUA—was a remarkable attempt by the Liberal government in the seventies to respond to city issues. Last week's Urban Affairs Conference at the University of Winnipeg devoted three sessions to a dozen speakers who talked about MSUA's birth in 1970, its accomplishments for a half-dozen years and its death.

> Michael Pitfield, now a senator but then Ottawa's most powerful bureaucrat, said the ministry-of-state concept arose out of the needed to create a focus on urban affairs without passing legislation to establish a full-fledged ministry.

> A further constraint was the British North America Act, which gives provinces the responsibility for cities. The truncated ministry would cope with the twin pressures of increasing interdependence (line departments often missed the essence of urban issues by simplifying them) and growing technology. It would formulate policies regarding cities but would not implement them.

> MSUA was an attempt to co-ordinate federal involvement in urban affairs, no small matter given the vast amount of property owned by the federal government, its thousands of employees and the myriad (often unexpected) effects on cities of tiny policy shifts.

In analysing the Conference John Sewell invoked Andre Saumier's description of the Ministry: "All brains, no brawn" and Tom Shoyama's comment: "Ottawa wasn't sure there was an urban crisis", as two elements at the opposite end of the spectrum. The real question in John Sewell's mind, and again stated by those who participated in the Seminar was "Is there a role for the federal government in urban policy?" John Sewell's column concludes:

> Should MSUA be reinvented or should some other vehicle be found? Should the federal Government just carry on without regard for a cohesive urban policy? Many at the conference leaned toward a positive answer to that last question.

In a sense the debate continues on the nature, scale and scope of urban problems in Canada. The fundamental source of 'the urban problems' is the process of urbanization itself. For perfectly rational and private and public economic reasons, people concentrate in Canadian cities in ever-increasing numbers and proportions as a matter of free choice. The consequences of these trends have generated problems, *of* the city, as well as *in* the city. Both problems share one common characteristic, they are highly inter-dependent. Housing is related to transportation and land use, and vice-versa. Land use and access to activities in all parts of the city affect the rich and the poor, they affect the revenues of the city as well as the natural environment and all of them loop back upon themselves in a continuing cause and effect chain. This realisation was noted by Mayor D.G. Newman when, as Chairman of the Canadian Federation of Mayors and Municipalities, he spoke at the first tri-level conference in 1972:

> The inter-relatedness of public policy is reflection of the inter-dependence of the social problems that policy tries to ameliorate. Unlike the rural society of the past, urban Canada is characterized by an incredible complex and inter-active pattern of social problems. This patternal problem, is to a great extent, the result of urban living and the pressures of increased urbanization.

This sense and reality of inter-dependence is at the core of Canada's urban problems and deserves continuing and thorough attention by Ottawa as well as the provincial capitals. The urban process is multi-dimensional, reaching back into the past and dealing with the future. That was the premise on which MSUA was created and that was the intention of its mandate and its operation, at least during the initial four years of its existence.

4

This publication is dedicated to an improved understanding of the urban decision-making process in Canada. The UBC Centre for Human Settlements acknowledges with gratitude the contribution of the authors who provided personal recollections of a significant Canadian experiment. We also acknowledge with appreciation the support of the Institute of Urban Studies at the University of Winnipeg which made it possible to publish this historic record.

Centre for Human Settlements
The University of British Columbia

SECTION ONE

ORIGINS

A LEGISLATIVE CHRONOLOGY

Arthur L. Fallick

Urbanization has become a pervasive phenomenon in Canada within the past two and a half decades. In slightly more than 100 years, an essentially rural society based on an agrarian economy has been transformed into an urban society with an industrial and resource-based economy.[1]

Recent census data indicate that cities and metropolitan areas in Canada comprise two-thirds of the approximately 25 million population. They constitute a dynamic, interdependent and highly interactive system which extends across the 5,000 mile width of the country, but which is concentrated within a 200-mile band to the north of the U.S. border. As a result, it is increasingly evident that not only are the majority of Canadians urban dwellers, but also, all Canadians depend on the urban system for economic, social and cultural growth. However, although the individual settlements within the national network are highly interactive across provincial boundaries, settlement policies and development strategies are constitutionally and institutionally a provincial responsibility.[2]

It has traditionally been part of Canada's conventional wisdom that the Federal Government had no legitimate business in the provincially dominated cities.[3] Conventional wisdom has also dictated that the infusion of money was the appropriate solution to problems both *of* and *in* the city.

As the subsequent chapters in this book reveal, herein lies a fundamental paradox of Canada's struggle to come to terms with its urban identity: the Federal Government has the power of "the purse" but little control over urban development; the provincial governments have constitutional power but often lack sufficient resources to address urban issues systematically; and the municpalities have the problems, but have neither the power nor the financial resources to systematically address the problems.[4] The effects of conventional wisdom, coupled with the constitutional paradox have militated against long-term solutions to Canada's urban problems.

Systematic attempts to understand and explain Canada's process of urbanization began to receive national examination in terms of policy formulation during the late 1960's. In particular, the creation of the Ministry of State for Urban Affairs as an instrument of Federal public policy designed to improve urbanization by co-ordinating the urban activities at the federal level and between Ottawa and the provinces, pioneered significant changes in approaches to Canadian urban public policy formulation and implementation. In the following chapters, people who were actively involved in the MSUA ''experiment'' provide a retrospective analysis of the efficacy of systematically aggregating policy responsibilities into a single federal ministry while leaving program delivery with line departments and primarily as a provincial responsibility.[5] The present overview provides a legislative chronology of the origins of MSUA and indicates some of the significant landmarks in the process leading up to the adoption of the Order-in-Council on July 1, 1971. This is followed by a discussion of the mandate which MSUA was given and the institutional structure which was developed to fulfill the mandate. This overview is intended also to provide the contextual logic which underlies the structure of the sub-sections and individual presentations in the book.

ORIGINS OF THE MINISTRY OF STATE FOR URBAN AFFAIRS

In the period between 1967 and 1979, a series of initiatives were undertaken which significantly influenced and altered fundamentally the ways in which the principal levels of government reacted to issues and problems affecting the city. They took place at a time when ''urban crises'' were the focus of national and international media attention, particularly in the U.S.A., and urban issues occupied a prominent position on political agenda.[6]

In the Canadian context, new directions in the evolution of federal-provincial strategies to cope with rapid urban development were established during the nation's centennial in 1967, and culminated in a speech from the throne in October 1970, in which the federal government set forth its plans to reorganize the urban activities under the direction of a Minister of State for Urban Affairs and Housing.[7] Details of the significant events leading to the creation of the Ministry of State are chronicled in Table 1.

This initiative was without precedent. It was the result of extensive studies by the federal government which felt increasingly compelled to consolidate its program impact on urban Canada and to marshall it on behalf of a systematic urban policy.[8] As a result of the 1970 Government Organization Act, the concept of Ministries of State was incorporated into the organizational structure of the federal government. This was, according to Crowley (1982), a period of "cooperative federalism", during which considerable attention was focussed on urban problems.[9] In 1971, the federal government response was to establish Ministries of State for Urban Affairs and for Science and Technology to deal with specific priority concerns to the government.[10] They were intended to have a limited life-span and be composed of highly technical and professional staff who were capable of long-term policy development. As Crowley suggests, "the Ministry of State concept was an innovative way of approaching what was essentially a problem of politics and coordination."[11]

Application of the Ministry of State Concept to Urban Affairs

MSUA was designed to be a policy ministry (policy as separated from program responsibilities), with a major research capacity which also included a consultative and co-ordination role vis-a-vis the provinces.[12] It was established inside the Canadian government decision-making process to co-ordinate and integrate federal initiative as a sectoral central policy agency.

In a report on the development, mandate, structure and functions of MSUA, Sunga and Duc (1975) suggest that other factors which motivated the creation of the Ministry included:

— the realization that the federal government was a major actor in urban Canada, notwithstanding the primacy of provincial and municipal governments in urban affairs;
— the recognition that the urban implications of federal activities needed to be understood more precisely, and that new policies and programs needed to be assessed in terms of both the urban objectives and

priorities of the Government of Canada, and of provincial and municipal aspirations for urban Canada;
— the fact that the national urban system is highly integrated and
responsive to policies at the national level;
— the realization that interdependent urban problems (housing, transportation, land use, environmental deterioration, fiscal pressures and
financial demands, among others) required comprehensive solutions
which would favorably influence the future pattern of urbanization and
the form and quality of urban regions;
— the recognition that policies and programs of all levels of government
require coordination to guide the development and enhance the quality
of life in existing and new urban centres.[13]

In summary, there was a growing recognition of the fact that urban
concerns impact on all levels of government and vice versa, and there
existed a need for intergovernmental consultation and coordination of
policies and programs affecting urban development in Canada. These,
and related issues are discussed in the first section of the book by H.P.
Oberlander and P.M. Pitfield.

TABLE 1

A CHRONICLE OF EVENTS LEADING TO THE CREATION OF THE MINISTRY OF STATE FOR URBAN AFFAIRS: 1967—1971

1967 — Centennial Year—concern with problems of rapid urbanization in
U.S.A. and Canada
— Federal Government increases participation in providing public
services to urban areas, and growing financial involvement through
urban renewal
— Provincial Governments increase focus on urban issues and problems
— Prime Minister Pearson convenes first federal-provincial conference
on housing and urban affairs resulting in establishment of Intergovernmental Committee on Urban and Regional Research
— Canadian Federation of Mayors and Municipalities unsuccessfully
attempt to gain legitimate decision-making role with the provincial
and federal governments
— Economic Council of Canada publishes ''The Canadian Economy
from the 1960's to the 1970's: Annual Review,'' with significant
emphasis on urban issues.

1968 — Science Council of Canada, Report No. 4, "Towards a National Science Policy for Canada", suggested the immediate planning of major projects in urban development and transportation

1969 — January 22—Report of the Hellyer Task Force on Housing and Urban Development which had been authorized by Cabinet on July 17, 1968.
— Hellyer resigned in May after the report recommendations were rejected by Cabinet
— June 3—Prime Minister Trudeau speaks to Canadian Federation of Mayors and Municipalities outlining the need for Federal initiative in solving urban development issues.
— Appointment of Robert Andras as Minister without portfolio responsible for Canada Mortgage and Housing Corporation.
— July—Robert Andras submits important memorandum to Cabinet suggesting policy alternatives regarding low-income Canadians, emphasizing that housing policy must flow from a broader understanding of urbanization.
— October—H. Lithwick commissioned by Canada Mortgage and Housing Corporation, begins major investigation of urbanization in Canada for Federal Government, based on Andras' request to study trends in urban development and the consequences if no active policy role is played by the Federal Government.

1970 — March—preliminary outline of Lithwick's analysis presented to Cabinet Committee on Priorities and Planning as attempt to achieve consensus on the nature of the urban problem.
— April—policy implications associated with the urban problem submitted by Lithwick. Two recommendations: (i) Federal agencies and departments should co-ordinate the impact of their policies and programs, (ii) one minister (Andras) should be designated to be the focal point for rationalizing urban-related federal activities.
— June 10—Andras speaks to Canadian Federation of Mayors and Municipalities advocating a department of urban affairs.
— October 8—Throne speech contains a proposal that MSUA be established.
— October 9—elaboration of MSUA concept by Prime Minister Trudeau during debate of the Throne Speech in the House of Commons.
— October Crisis War Measures Act.
— December 9—concept of MSUA translated into legislation as part of the Government Organization Act (Bill C-207, section 14).

1971 — April—meeting in Winnipeg by representatives from the three levels

of government to prepare for an initial tri-level conference.
— May—Government Organization Act passed through Parliament
— June 28—Proclamation creating MSUA approved
— July 1—After 3-hour debate, the Question is put and the Order-in-Council adopted. MSUA exists.

The Mandate of the Ministry

The proclamation of the Governor in Council stipulated that the Minister should formulate and develop policies for implementation through measures *within* fields of federal jurisdiction in respect of:

— the most appropriate means by which the Government of Canada may have a beneficial influence on the evolution of the process of urbanization in Canada;
— the integration of urban policy with other policies and programs of the Government of Canada; and
— the fostering of cooperative relationships in respect of urban affairs with the provinces and, through them, their municipalities, and with the public and with private organizations.

In order to fulfill its mandate, the Ministry was accorded wide-ranging powers, duties and functions associated with the development of urban policies and programs, the coordination of federal urban activity with the urban initiatives of other levels of government, and the establishment of urban research, advice and recommendations to ensure consistency between policies and objectives over a broad spectrum of urban issues which involve a number of federal, provincial and municipal agencies.[14] For example, in the area of policy development, the Minister was empowered to:

(i) *initiate* proposals for *new policies*, projects and activities;
(ii) *evaluate* proposals for *new policies*, projects and activities and seek to ensure their consistency with federal urban policies;
(iii) *evaluate existing policies*, projects and activities of the Government of Canada that have an influence on urban affairs and recommend changes therein where required;
(iv) where appropriate, *participate in projects* and activities of the Government of Canada that may have an influence on urbanization in Canada; and
(v) seek, in consultation with other authorities concerned, *the cooperative development* of urban policy in Canada.

The Ministry developed a conceptual framework through which federal policy objectives were articulated in the areas of urban growth and distribution, urban economy, urban land and space, urban service systems, urban environment, urban information, urban planning/ interventions, and urban institutions. The result was the formulation of a national urban policy framework supportive of the urban thrusts of the provincial and municipal governments.[15]

MSUA's coordination mandate had two distinct but interrelated components which involved linking the objectives and initiatives of other federal departments (interdepartmental), and also liaising with the other levels of government (interdepartmental). The Minister was given the power to:

> (i) *coordinate, promote* and *recommend* national policies in respect of urban affairs among departments and agencies of the Government of Canada;
> (ii) *coordinate* the *activities* of the Government of Canada in establishing cooperative relationships with the provinces and their municipalities for the enhancement of the urban environment; and
> (iii) *coordinate* the involvement of the Government of Canada with *other* governments and non-government organizations in urban policy matters.

Specifically, this involved keeping the various federal agencies apprised of the urban dimensions and consequences of their activities, and at the same time, establishing close collaboration with provincial governments and municipal authorities to identify urban programs which had a direct bearing on federal urban initiatives, as well as determining how the federal initiatives could best be tailored to local circumstances and priorities. Details of the complex nature of this coordinative function are provided in the second section of the book through the contributions by Andre Saumier, Victor Goldbloom and Desmond Newman.

The third substantial dimension of the Ministry's mandate authorized the Minister to:

> (i) *initiate research* and policy studies relating to urbanization;
> (ii) *coordinate*, in cooperation with other departments and agencies of the Government of Canada, *research relating to urbanization* that has been undertaken or financed by those departments or agencies; and
> (iii) *recommend priorities* for research in urbanization.

The research function was designed to be both pragmatic and flexible by advancing practical concepts and solutions to urban problems. As Sunga and Duc suggest:

"MSUA's research program is concerned with such fundamental problems as explaining the structures and processes that shape the distribution of activities within cities, providing a more inclusive account of the key components and their interrelationships within urban regions, and securing a clearer understanding of the national urban system"[16]

The research was conducted through five directorates: Program Evaluation; Urban Environment and Economy; Urban Growth and Land; Information Systems; and Urban Institutions and Services. In particular, major research activities focussed on land use, housing, transportation and communications, environmental quality, population mobility, social development and economic growth.

In the third section of the book, the contributions by Wellar and Jackson vividly illustrate the dynamic interrelationships between the Ministry's mandate and the organizational structure which was established to achieve its stated objectives. Their recollections stem from their respective roles in the policy and research, and priorities and planning branches of the Ministry (See Figure 1) and reveal the effectiveness and the constraints which characterized the Ministry's proposed coordination of federal interagency and intergovernmental urban initatives through its research, evaluative and policy development functions.

In the final section, the successes and failures of MSUA are discussed within the broader context of urban public policy in Canada. Len Gertler and Peter Oberlander raise provocative issues about the continuing need for systematic approaches to urban affairs by the three levels of government. In challenging the efficacy of current strategies, these two polemics attempt to raise urban issues once again to a position of prominence on the political agenda.

NOTES

1. Oberlander, H.P., "In Praise of Cities: What is Canada's Urban Future?" Paper presented to Vancouver Institute, January 19, 1974.
2. Oberlander, H.P. and A.L. Fallick, (eds.). "Intermediate Settlements: Planning and Management Within A Spatial Strategy". Proceedings of

a Seminar of Experts: *Planning and Management Within a Spatial Strategy.* Prepared for the Eighth Session of the United Nations Commission on Human Settlements, Kingston, Jamaica. 1985.

3. Oberlander, "In Praise."

4. Oberlander, H.P., "Submerged Third" *Policy Options*, July, 1986, p. 33-35.

5. According to Shaffenburg, P.M. Pitfield described MSUA as an experiment because it would function horizontally on problems of urbanization, across the range of urban agencies, but without the normal types of territorial prerogatives. Shaffenburg, A.A., "The Development of Federal Urban Policy: A Case Study of MSUA, 1971-1977." Unpublished M.A. thesis, University of Waterloo, 1978. See also, Pitfield, P.M. "The Shape of Government in the 1980's: Techniques and Instruments for Policy Formulation at the Federal Level," *Canadian Public Administration*, 19 (April, 1976), 8-20.

6. The context within which MSUA was established has been addressed by A. O'Brien, A.D. Doerr and R.W. Crowley in articles published in The Canadian Journal of Regional Science, v.1.(1982). In addition, background information on the role of MSUA in the formulation of Canadian urban policy has been derived from D.M. Cameron's chapter in *Issues in Canadian Public Policy* edited by G. Bruce Doern and V. Seymour Wilson, Macmillan, 1974, and from A.A. Shaffenburg, op. cit.

7. Canada. Speech from the Throne, October 8, 1970. This was followed by the Organization Act, December 9, 1970, presented to the House of Commons as Bill C-207, which heralded in the Ministry of State for Urban Affairs (July, 1971), and the Ministry of State for Science and Technology (August, 1971)

8. Oberlander's speech to Vancouver Institute, op. cit., identifies three essentially Canadian problems which prompted the creation of MSUA. They were: the pervasive nature of urbanization which demanded examination to determine rational policies; the constitutional impediments to federal urban change strategies; and the proliferation of Federal programs dealing with specific aspects of urban life which were beyond the constitutional limitations.

9. Crowley, E.W., "The Design of Government Policy Agencies: Do We Learn from Experience?" *Canadian Journal of Regional Science*, V.1, 1982, P. 104-123.

10. Under the 1978 Ministries and Ministry of State Act, the Ministry of State for Economic Development was created in 1979, and the Ministry of State for Science and Technology in 1980.

11. Crowley, "Design", p. 106.

12. A review of the internal organization of MSUA is contained in Doerr,

16

A.D., ''Organizing for Urban Policy: Some comments on MSUA'', The Canadian Journal of Regional Sciences, v.1., 1982, p. 97.

13. P.S. Sunga and G.A. Duc, ''MSUA and the federal government'', Canada, Ministry of State, Urban Affairs, 1975, A-75-1 Urban Paper.

14. Canada, MSUA, ''The Federal Urban Domain'' vol. 3, ''Nature and Urban Implications of Selected Federal Programs,'' Discussion Paper B. 73-12. Planning and Evaluation Division, Program Evaluation and Advice Section.

15. Sunga and Duc, ''MSUA and the federal government,'' p.6.

16. Ibid.; p.8.

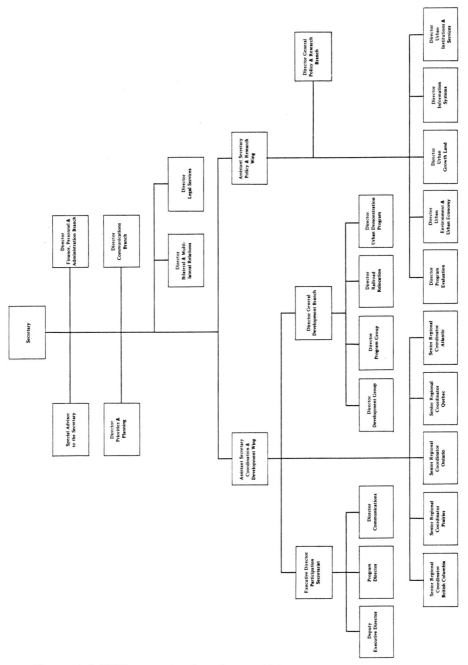

Figure 1 MSUA organization chart, 1974.

NAVIGATING THROUGH SHOALS: HOW TO CREATE A MINISTRY WHILE OPERATING IT

H. PETER OBERLANDER

The Constitution Act of 1981 and the British North America Act 1867 before it, allocates the power to govern Canada between the 10 pronvinces and one federal government. There is no Constitutional recognition of local government, and matters covered by 'property and civil rights' as well as those of 'local concern' are assigned to provincial jurisdiction.Consequently, Federal involvement in solving emerging urban problems from housing to infrastructure, from urban renewal to rapid transit, have been tentative and built on a slim legislative base.

This reluctance of becoming involved in matters that are provincial constitutionally is borne out by the following resume of events starting with an historic Order in Council in 1918 under the then prevailing War Measures Act. During the ensuing 70 years the government in Ottawa has legislated its way into urban affairs, always looking over its shoulder to see when and how much the provinces would object.

FEDERAL GOVERNMENT INVOLVEMENT IN URBAN AFFAIRS DURING THE FIRST HALF-CENTURY: 1918—1967

1918 Order-in-Council for federal financial assistance to the provinces to provide for housing (December 3; tabled in the House February 27, 1919); War Measures Act (1918) used to implement the Order-in-Council.

1935 Dominion Housing Act (An Act to assist the Construction of Houses); Commons Committee on Housing.

1937 Home Improvement Guarantee Act.

1938 National Housing Act.

1939 Central Mortgage Bank proposed; Wartime Housing Ltd., an interim agency, established.

1941 Wartime Housing Act; National Building Code (advisory only).

1942 Veterans Land Act; Home Extension Plan.

1944 Curtis Report (Special Committee on Postwar Reconstruction) Vol. IV, Housing and Community Planning—called for a recognition of the role of government, particularly the federal government, in the housing field. It also recommended that a Dominion Town Planning Agency be established to promote and coordinate town planning throughout the country.[1]

1945 NHA Amendment "Central Mortgage and Housing Corporation—Discounting Facilities".

1946 The establishment of Central Mortgage and Housing Corporation.

1949 NHA Amendments "Providing for joint operation of housing projects and loans to home owners"—(Section 35)—Federal-provincial partnership in land assembly (75%-25%) and public housing.

1953 NHA Amendment "Substitution of new legislation to ensure approved lenders, etc."—allowed grants to municipalities for urban renewal areas being redeveloped for any federal, provincial or municipal public purposes as well as low cost rental housing.

1954 National Housing Act.

1956 NHA Amendment "Provision for Contribution to Municipalities, Home Loans, Housing Research, etc.."

1960 NHA Amendment "Provision for Contribution to Municipalities, Home Loans, Housing Research, etc.."

1964 NHA Amendment "Respecting renewal programs, public housing projects, etc."—provincial authority in the housing field.

1967 Federal-Provincial Conference on Housing and Urban Development—Dec. first such conference, convened by Prime Minister L.B. Pearson.

1968 Pierre Elliot Trudeau elected Prime Minister.

This resume, however, ignores the all-pervasive and rapidly growing federal presence in the cities through its vast land holdings including harbours and airports, as well as massive public works and buildings for the public services such as post offices, tax department, agriculture and regional economic development. This presence had been expanding during the post-war decades, resulting in a strategic and large-scale impact on the nature and quality of Canadian cities.

Suburban Canada, the country's more characteristic result of post war urbanization, was built by CMHC through its programs and financial incentives and supports. The resume however, also suggests that federal government intervention in urban affairs has come at times of national crises or upheaval: following both world wars, during the depression and finally after belated recognition that events of the 1960's were having a greater impact on urban areas than the earlier crises.

The concentration on housing legislation reflects the fact that federal involvement in the urban field tended to regard crises in urban areas as linear, normally economic problems "solved" by single purpose and often short run programs. Not until the concentration of studies in the latter half of the 1960's did the idea gain currency that programs designed to solve certain problems—normally without benefit of suitable research or policy analysis—were in fact frequently creating new problems.

The felt need to use the War Measures Act to implement the first federal urban legislation underlines the most important aspect of federal interventions in the urban area, that of federal-provincial jurisdictions. The linear approach of solving housing, or the larger urban issues, project by project, or problem by problem, was challenging established techniques and institutions. In the late 1960's, the most important challenge was political. Pierre Elliot Trudeau became Prime Minister in 1968 with a resounding mandate and a new agenda and committed himself and his Cabinet to:

— a strong federal government within federal jurisdiction, exercising determined leadership vis-a-vis the ten provinces
— governing by objectives through articulated goals, anticipating the future and evaluating performance
— a rational and systematic approach to legislative and administrative processes.

These ideas reflected Trudeau's explicit belief that Canada is more than the sum of its 10 provinces and 2 territories and that Canada's unity and future were to be served by a federal government acting for all Canadians on matters of pervasive concern.

How Do You Create An Agency While Operating It?

MSUA's early months have often been compared to building a boat, one plank at a time while running down a raging white water river, dodging rocks and eddys while simultaneously laying the keel, and frantically inserting oars where possible. During these proceedings the crew gets badly shaken, one or two are lost overboard and all of them are drenched. But gradually the boat is built; the water is sealed out and it navigates successfully around the more dangerous shoals, reaching downstream with most of its cargo intact—at least for a while.

MSUA's early day-to-day struggle with concepts, ideas, and administrative procedures are perhaps best glimpsed from fragments of the running record kept by the office of the Secretary of MSUA during the early months of 1971.

Trudeau's first administration provided a context and framework for a substantial and substantive shift in dealing with urban affairs nationally. The need for change and the neccessity for action was widely accepted and is best foreshadowed in Robert Andras' speech shortly after being appointed to the Cabinet as Minister without Portfolio responsible for CMHC in 1969.

The Constitution can serve in a manner that facilitates the actions and changes we need in planning the future of our cities. If our institutional forms are inadequate, let us seek to discover and develop institutional forms which will do the job.[2]

The 1970 Speech from the Throne, read on October 8, contained the first public indication of the federal government's intention to establish a special new mechanism to deal with urban affairs:

It is estimated that eighty percent of the population of Canada will be resident in a few large cities by the end of this century. By comparison with the recent past, this is a new accumulation of problems. . . . To foster coordination of the activities of all levels of government and contribute to sound urban growth and development, the Government proposes the re-organization of its urban activities under the direction of a Minister of State for Urban Affairs and Housing. The Government seeks, by making rational its efforts in these fields, and through consultation with those most directly concerned, to help Canadians reach and implement the decisions that will determine their urban future.[3]

Although the Throne Speech did not indicate the characteristics of a "Minister of State" or whether the appointment of such a minister in charge of "urban affairs and housing" also involved the establishment of some type of federal agency, during the Throne Speech debate the Prime Minister elaborated on the Minister of State concept:

These ministers of state generally will be responsible for developing new and comprehensive federal policies in areas where the development of such policies is of particular urgency and importance. The mandates of these ministers will be of a temporary nature, of such a duration as to enable them to come to grips with the policy problems assigned to them. They will not generally have departments, but only relatively small secretariats with no program responsibilities. The new system will give to the Prime Minister more flexibility in assigning senior ministers to tackle important problems that require policy development.[4]

Only on October 22 did the PCO describe in somewhat more detail Ministers of State. There would be two categories: the Minister of State, to be identical to—and replace—the existing Minister without Portfolio and, secondly, the Minister of State (for designated purpose) who would:

. . . be responsible for agencies of the government. The "secretariat" (*not* "ministry" or "department") of the minister of state (for designated purpose) would include the normal complement of exempt staff plus a group, probably between 30 or 50 officers primarily concerned with policy formulation. . . . Although the requirements of ministers of state (for designated purpose) might vary from one minister to another, these ministers will not in principle carry program responsibilities, even though they might have a Crown Corporation reporting to them. These ministers might, however, have a fairly significant coordinating responsibility not only within the federal government but with the provinces.[5]

In a letter of October 23 to Mr. Andras, the Prime Minister reiterated these characteristics and added that the temporary nature of the mandate meant that it could be abandoned, be maintained for an indefinite period or, in a succeeding government organization, become a department.[6]

During the Throne Speech debate Robert Andras was named Minister-designate for the proposed Ministry, as well as for CMHC and the NCC, and Dr. H. Peter Oberlander was appointed Secretary-designate.

From these early indications it is clear that MSUA was designed to be an experiment in public administration, by assigning it an exclusive policy development mandate, thereby separating policy from programs and the Ministry of State from line departments. Policy development also was to include emphasis on co-ordinating both inter-departmental and inter-governmental agencies and consulting with "those most directly concerned", a slight hint at involving the municipalities.

As a politically fragile and administratively sensitive experiment, MSUA, both as an idea and as a viable political structure, was put to the test almost before it was even created.

The proposed new organizational mechanism naturally required the adoption of new legislation to establish the form *per se*. Government planning was severely disrupted, however, from October 21 to almost the end of the year by the October crisis in Quebec. However, first reading was given to the Government Organization Act, on December 9, 1970. Part IV of the proposed Act was the Ministries and Ministers of State Act (An Act respecting the organization of the Government of Canada and Matters related or incidental thereto (Bill C-207)). Second reading was given on January 26, 1971, but the Bill's anticipated rapid passage through Parliament was delayed at this point. On the one hand, the opposition considered that the proposed method of creating Ministries would give too much power to the government since it would be able both to establish and terminate Ministries without reference to Parliament. On the other hand and with specific reference to the proposed urban affairs and housing ministry, a second argument, summarized by T.C. Douglas in the House, was raised:

Housing and urban affairs is not a temporary matter. If the government sets up a Ministry of housing and urban affairs, I serve notice that in my opinion it will be complete violation of clause 14 Part IV of this Bill.[7]

Successive delays in passing Bill C-207 had obvious repercussions for the proposed Ministry since it meant that it did not formally exist and thus had no constitutional or institutional jurisdiction for a much longer period of time than originally anticipated. For legal and constitutional reasons the Ministry could not be established by the passing of an Act of Parliament. The simple reason for this is that an Act involves starting with something tangible, for example, a program, which is to be undertaken. Such was not the case, however, for an organization which was to be set up to produce something tangible (policies) after its own establishment.

The Minister had written to Michael Pitfield of the PCO in mid-December 1970 raising the question of preparing a draft of the order-in-council to create the Ministry. No action appears to have been taken until late January when Bill C-207 was expected to pass within six weeks, and drafting was begun by the Ministry. By the beginning of April a reasonably comprehensive statement was available. But there was still the legal dilemma of the form the legislation should take. Eventually the unique and original device of the Proclamation was developed by the Secretary, Mr. Saumier, and Messrs. Krupka, Gallant, and Pitfield of the PCO.

For legal reasons the Proclamation would require the unanimous consent of Parliament. Allan MacEachen, the government House leader, attempted to win support for a unanimous resolution, but the opposition began to want to open the debate to a discussion of urban issues. In fact, there were four key points on which passage of the reorganization bill through the House was impeded. First, there was confusion throughout the House concerning the differences between a policy and a program agency. Secondly, there were feelings that the government was attempting to circumvent the constitution, both in the introduction of the Ministry of State concept and in this federal intervention in urban affairs. Thirdly, the opposition wanted a Bill for the new Ministry to be brought before the House, on which it would then have a debate on urban issues. Finally, the above points conjoined to produce an increasingly negative feeling towards the Ministry of State concept within the government itself.

Ultimately, Ivo Krupka of the PCO suggested another legal device which could be used to have the Proclamation passed by Parliament. Instead of a positive resolution, which would require unanimous consent of the House, a negative resolution, a rarely used device, could be introduced. This would require that after the order-in-council was tabled the House would have three days in which to register opposition— but not debate. If, however, ten or more members were against the resolution, it would then have to be debated within twenty-four hours, a requirement which would force the opposition to be publicly identified. After a month of considering whether to introduce a negative resolution, use of this device was accepted. As a result, when introduced in the House on the night of June 28th the Proclamation was quickly passed by unanimous consent. Finally, third reading of the bill was passed on May 26, 1971, opening the way for the official establishment of the new Ministry before the end of the session. The order-in-council was entered in the orders of the day on June 25. The Proclamation was debated and approved in the House on the night of June 28, signed by the Governor-General on June 30 and gazetted on July 10.[8]

Two footnotes, in a sense, to the legal-constitutional problems encountered in developing the Proclamation deserve mention here: the Ministry's title and the French version of the Proclamation.

In the Throne Speech the government had announced that there would be a Minister of State for "Urban Affairs and Housing". During discussion prior to the Throne Speech between Mr. Andras and Michael Pitfield, this title had been favoured. After his arrival, Dr.

Oberlander felt that the title should be "Urban Affairs" only since housing was merely one aspect of urban affairs; housing was basically a provincial matter and therefore should not be emphasized in the title of a federal agency, and the Minister for Urban Affairs might not always be the Minister responsible for CMHC. Thus in December, Mr. Andras advised Pitfield that the title "Minister of State for Urban Affairs" would be "A better description of the research and policy development and coordination mandate across a complex inter-related range of federal activities without direct program responsibility." Until almost the end, however, neither Mr. Drury nor the PCO was convinced of the validity of the "Urban Affairs" title, particularly since it had not been used in the Throne Speech. Agreement was reached with the opposition the night before the Proclamation was introduced that the title "Urban Affairs" would be acceptable.

Discussions concerning the Proclamation and its drafting had been in English. Thus it was not until mid-June, after the final version of the Proclamation had been confirmed and the translation into French completed, that Mr. Saumier discovered certain words and phrases had been incorrectly translated, including, most notoriously, "une politique urbaine" rather than "des politiques concernant l'urbanisation". Mr. Saumier's rewrite of this translation plus complaints to the PCO resulted in the errors persisting, but in a different and preferable version of the Proclamation being gazetted than was signed as the order-in-council. The final aspect of this unfortunate occurrence was the realization in July that the Ministry's French title should be "Ministere d'Etat aux Affairs urbaines" rather than "Department d'Etat charge des Affairs urbaines", which had been used.

The allocation of governmental responsibilities, political and economic, was established at Confederation when Canada was an agrarian economy and a rural society. Since then, Canada has become an urban society based on an industrial economy, in which an exponentially growing number of economic, social and political issues emerge and are manifest at the municipal level. The prevailing governmental structures and related strategies for addressing urban affairs reflects historic perceptions.

At Confederation, the founding provinces had a scattered and agrarian population, whose collective needs were few, hence requiring very limited public policies and services. One hundred and twenty years later, Canada's reality is a network of cities and towns, interactive and interdependent with pressing demands for public policies and actions. It was within this context thatMSUA was conceived and its structure delineated. With the demise of the Ministry, the disparity which exists in Canada between urban reality and political power is once again apparent.

NOTES

1. Special Committee on Postwar Reconstruction, Housing and Community Planning, Vol.4, (Ottawa: King's Printer, 1946), p.16
2. Notes for an Address by the Honourable Robert Andras to the CFMM, Ottawa, June 3, 1969, p.11
3. House of Commons Debates, Speech from the Throne, October 8, 1970, p.2.
4. House of Commons Debates, October 9, 1970, p.36
5. PCO, Memorandum, "The Ministry of State System", October 22, 1970, (File C-100-8-1)
6. Trudeau, P.E., Letter to Mr. Andras, October 23, 1970, (File S-2010-1)
7. House of Commons Debates, March 31, 1971, p.4789
8. The Canada Gazette, Part I, Vol. 105, No. 28, July 10, 1971, (Ottawa: Queen's Printer). pp. 1768-70

THE ORIGINS OF THE MINISTRY OF STATE

P.M. Pitfield

The Ministry of State was not, as some would have you believe, a theoretical conception secretly nurtured in the Privy Council Office and suddenly launched, full blown, on an unsuspecting government and public. It was a mechanism that developed in an evolutionary manner during the '60s and '70s to meet a series of needs that became increasingly evident as, first, Mr. Pearson, then, Mr. Trudeau went about the business of governing.

These needs resulted from the more pro-active stance of governments in the years following the Second World War and consequential growth in the size, scope and complexity of government. The implicit assumption of pro-activity was that government had objectives it was trying to achieve, policies that would serve those objectives and programs that expressed those policies. This is obvious today but in the early '60s it was a new way of looking at things and it was the Glassco Commission that first really drove the message home.

But the Glassco Commission was confined to the administrative side of things and looked more at what government was in the '50s than at what it was to become in the '60s and '70s. The task of fitting administrative to political decision-making was left, first, to Mr. Pearson and, then, to Mr. Trudeau. It was a job enormously complicated by the sudden and explosive growth of technology and interdependence that continue to be the hallmark of our times.

In approaching these requirements Mr. Pearson and Mr. Trudeau each made it very clear that decision-making reforms had to be consistent with fundamental constitutional principles and, to the greatest possible degree, an evolutionary development of established political and administrative institutions. In other words, for example, ministerial and collective responsibility were to be rigorously observed, on the one hand, and the equilibrium between the roles of Parliament, Ministers and civil servants maintained, on the other hand.

It would have been infinitely easier politically and much less intellectually demanding to proceed in dramatic strokes with the presidential Prime Ministership and politicized public service that the governments' opponents were bound to allege in any event, did in fact allege with great indignation, and now seem to have implemented themselves without much adverse comment. But this was a course both Mr. Pearson and Mr. Trudeau were extremely anxious to avoid and rightly so, for they foresaw correctly the fundamental damage such an approach would do not only to the coherence of their Governments, much less to the credibility of government generally but, more fundamentally and irrevocably, to the very nature of our democratic institutions.

In any event, central to any reform of the Government's decision-making processes in the '60s was the manner of the involvement of elected politicians in the Administration. For decades the size and the complexity of government had been growing, but until the late '50s the number of politicians at the interface between the administration and the people had remained comparatively static. Then, starting with Mr. Diefenbaker, there was a gradual growth in the number of Ministers, and the question facing Mr. Pearson was whether to reverse this process or,—if it was stopped or allowed to continue—how to organize the Executive so as to more efficiently and effectively perform its functions?

As one who had been a career civil servant, Mr. Pearson felt strongly that the number of elected politicians in the Administration had to increase: to better speak for the regions of the country, to better represent at the Cabinet level the increasing number of issues before the Government and to better supervise the growing bureaucracy. For a time he tried to organize his Cabinet on a tiered basis along the lines used by the British. This would have ultimately permitted fewer departments, thus reducing turmoil amongst—and increased expenditure in—the public service, with a small Cabinet of only the most senior Ministers supported by a larger number of 'junior' Ministers who would not be "of the Cabinet".

These efforts were quickly shown to be too revolutionary. They gave rise to in-fighting amongst his followers and feelings in many parts of the country who felt they were getting 'second best' in a junior Minister. It was concluded that an overtly tiered Cabinet would not work in Canada's federal system. Consequently, Mr. Pearson opted for a larger Ministry all of whom would be in the Cabinet, but all of whom would be correlated through organization and process to differentiated roles. Senior Ministers would lead in the various policy areas and in the major central agency functions but, at least in their policy areas, every Minister would be a senior Minister. Thus, two objectives were served: first, the policy areas were given greater coherence and definition; second, in the senior co-ordinating committee of Ministers—Priorities and Planning—the seeds were sown for the gradual evolution in Canada of what amounted to an 'inner' Cabinet, and that is what has happened with surprising rapidity and public acceptance.

There were of course a host of detailed developments in all of this. Other things were being done and the consequences of all these changes registered across the entire system of government. My reason for giving this background is that it is the context in which the concept of the Ministry of State developed.

The Ministry of State was needed for two purposes: first, in order to effectively rationalize the division of responsibilities amongst Ministers and, second, to effectively represent at the Cabinet level national concerns previously reflected only as an aspect of some other, often less consequential, policy area.

With regard to the effective rationalization of the division of responsibilities amongst Ministers, both Mr. Diefenbaker and Mr. Pearson tried to use the office of Minister without Portfolio to concentrate responsibility for a particular area of policy or program. This could not be made to work. It could not work because although in political terms responsibilities could be confided to a Minister without Portfolio, in legal terms a Minister without Portfolio could never be more than an adviser. He or she could not have the control and management of public servants or even receive responsibility for crown corporations or agencies under the Public Service Transfer and Rearrangement of Duties Act. This was because it was held by the Department of Justice that a Minister without Portfolio was not the holder of an ''office'' under the terms of that act. Thus, a Minister without Portfolio would always be in that special political and constitutional purgatory: responsibility without authority.

With regard to the effective representation at the Cabinet level of national concerns otherwise reflected only as an aspect of other policy areas, this of course was one of the purposes for which both Mr. Diefenbaker and Mr. Pearson had already sought to use the Minister without Portfolio. But where in their times the requirement had been essentially only one of giving political profile and demonstrating government sensitivity, by the mid-'60s the need was also increasingly real in terms of policy formulation, administrative follow-through, and bureaucratic supervision. The use of Ministers without Portfolio was shown to be wholly inadequate for these purposes. Rationalization would have to be done by a specific statutory enactment and these the Opposition would be bound to filibuster, as in fact it always did.

Hence, the Minister of State concept was introduced by the Government Organization Act of 1969. It permits two forms of organization.

The first and simplest is the appointment by the Governor General of a Minister very similar to the old Minister without Portfolio but with the decisive difference that a Minister of State can receive the power to manage programs and direct civil servants that other Ministers have. This office has been used a great deal in every subsequent Administration and has proven to be very useful.

The second form provides not simply for a Minister but also for a Secretariat led by a Deputy Head and including civil servants. This can be immediately secured by order-in-council but must be ratified following a three-day debate in Parliament. To underline that the Ministry of State, as this device is called, is not intended to be used to form permanent line departments there is also a provision which allows its dissolution in the same manner as its formation, namely: by proclamation of the Governor-in-Council.

The Ministry of State technique was used three times by the Trudeau Administration and once by Mr. Clark's government.

Two of the Ministries of State—those for Social (MSSD) and for Economic Policy (MSERD)—had to do with the co-ordination of large policy areas where there were already numerous departments involved in competing and often more or less contradictory programs. Social Policy included the activities of at least nine departments; Economic Policy, which really meant micro-economic policy, had about seventeen departments in play. The job of co-ordination was clearly enormous. Previously, it was a job Finance, the Treasury Board and, increasingly the major, or "lead", department in the policy area had tried to do—as they are again trying to do now—but this approach, which worked well in simpler times, had been shown to have several severe failings in more complex ones. To itemize only the major failings:

First, it greatly constrains the in-put of the concerned Ministers into decision-making;

Second, it puts the two financial central agencies into the position of being the actual decision-makers, with very little right of appeal;

Third, because the Minister of Finance and the President of the Treasury Board are already over-burdened, it means that the decision-making is actually done by officials—often at the third and fourth level;

Fourth, to the extent that this is off-set by giving leadership to the major department, it inevitably distorts both priorities and expenditure in favour of that department;

Fifth, the cumulative effect of these devices is not only to encourage confusion and contradiction between policies and programs, but also leaves Ministers and officials in other departments in the dark about what is going on and thus, unable to compensate for or defend decisions.

All of these factors flawed the present Government's recent decision on, and defense of, its moves with regard to old age pensions. In previous Administrations such errors could have resulted in the demise of the Minister, if not of the Government itself. But that is only to speak of the short term political effects. The longer term consequences are far more serious. Because the Government has had to retreat in disorder, the direction of policy development and the allocation of funds and, inevitably, of manpower, are in chaos. A key Minister is discredited and a vital area of policy demanding review is less tractable. The Government's freedom of maneouvre has been greatly reduced not only in social policy but also across the whole macro-economy. Throughout the whole sad story lurks the suspicion that extremely significant matters of public policy are being determined in only one part of the Government and, probably, deep in the bowels of the bureaucracy.

The Ministry of State system goes far to avoid these failings. It is not without failings of its own, but these can be avoided without great difficulty. The most important of them have to do with their propensity to breed bureaucracies of their own, to complicate process, and to drift into pure transactional politics. But the essence of good public administration is preventing such pitfalls. Where the first prototype, MSERD, did not come to grips with them until too late, the last to be tried—MSSD—stayed small and focused. It pioneered in tracing the social policy consequences of government expenditures. Its work was both unprecedented and extremely revealing.

By thus threatening to challenge the received wisdom of the central agencies in a climate where the short-comings of MSERD were widely perceived, MSSD became an easy target when Mr. Turner was looking around for high profile candidates for elimination to symbolize his differences with the Trudeau regime. Both MSERD and MSSD got the chop. Few wept. Fewer still paused to wonder how coordination of the policy areas would be done, how public and accountable the process would be.

The two remaining Ministries of State had to do with science policy and urban affairs. These two share several characteristics:

They are both aspects of the policies of a great many other departments, involve the expenditures of a great deal of money and are deeply involved in matters of primarily provincial jurisdiction. They are both vital to our quality of life and economic wellbeing, to our future, and to the basics of decision-making—the one, because scientific concerns permeate so many questions of public policy and the other, because the urban community is where government is closest to the people.

Of the two, MOSST is the only one to survive. Yet, in many ways, it has been the most disappointing of the Ministries of State and therein lies a tale of the vagaries of politics.

From the politician's point of view, the difficulty of the Ministry of State system has always been its lack of clout in program terms. To be an effective coordinator of others it was felt that Ministries of State must be confined to policy formulation and not have programs of their own to nurture. That this lack of crass political currency can be off-set in a government where process is well-defined and backed up by Prime Ministerial support became increasingly evident towards the end of the Trudeau years, but at the beginning Ministers of State were consumed by the pursuit of programs to demonstrate their importance and to build political followings. None was more focused in this direction than was MOSST and, consequently, rather than seeking to develop the advisory capacity to play in the inter-departmental policy process, at the ministerial and official levels, great effort, time and credibility were expended in trying to take over territory from other departments. The tree grows as the twig is bent and MOSST has never regained its lost opportunities.

And the opportunities were there. MOSST had grown out of years of effort to introduce science policy into the senior levels of decision-making. Various forms of science advisors and secretariats had been tried, ultimately in the very offices of the Prime Minister and the Privy Council. The conclusion that science needed a Minister of its own was painfully arrived at and, indeed, constituted part of the rationale for Ministries of State. When the way was finally clear, the opportunity was missed in large part because of primordial concern for constitutional principles and for evolution rather than revolution: concern for a Minister's right to determine the fulfillment of his mandate, on the one hand; concern, on the other, for the gradual development of relations with other departments and central agencies, for avoiding the vigorous imposition of a pre-conceived pattern for how responsible people are to work together.

To be sure there were other factors besides the pursuit of clout and failure to lay down the law. Advisers with the excellence to impress the scientific community and the skills to manage a political process are notoriously hard to find; and, organization for scientific input is a conundrum no less in the private sector than it is in the public one. But all these difficulties were not very different from those encountered in urban affairs. Yet, in its short life, MSUA went far to overcome them.

The Ministry of State for Urban Affairs was a novel approach to a typically Canadian dilemma: on the one hand, under the Constitution, municialities are an area of provincial jurisdiction and the provinces are more than ever determined that this should remain so; on the other hand, as the federal government has grown bigger and more complex, its relationships with municipalities have multiplied in number and impact far beyond what the Fathers of Confederation ever envisaged. A host of programs having to do with economic and social development such as employment, youth training, regional development, and so forth, entail municipal expenditure. Proportionately smaller but still very large sums are spent more directly on such matters as housing and federal works of all kinds. The consequences of the constitutional dilemma in this situation was to encourage an almost total lack of planning and co-ordination in terms of urban impact, with incredible costs to efficiency and effectiveness at all levels of government.

In this situation, thinking such as Jane Jacob's "Economy of Cities" led to the conclusion that a designated Minister, at the federal level, with authority over CMHC, the NCC and the urban aspects of other major government policies and programs, and with the help of a small staff, would be perceived as a desirable reform. Initially it was, but soon its only public advocates were professionals in the field. When their expectations were not immediately realized, they too began to carp.

And, they had lots of company. In the context of the federal-provincial situation at the time, the Provinces quickly rejected any effort by the federal government to put its own house in order as an intervention in provincial affairs. The federal bureaucracy was opposed to: officials with a categorical urban mandate because they objected to increased Ministerial direction; Ministers and officials whose policies and programs were affected by major urban implications because their more fundamental purposes were further complicated. The recruitment of officials, expert in the area and capable of leading the evolution of relationships with the interests involved,—was inevitably difficult. Politicians and officials at the municipal level who at first were inclined to be enthusiastic were scared off by provincial opposition and apparent lack of federal determination.

Thus, from its very beginnings, MSUA laboured under heavy disadvantages. Nonetheless, viewed from within the government, its credibility and effectiveness developed surprisingly quickly. It contributed substantially to the shaping of policies and programs indirectly involving urban affairs. It played an increasingly important consultative role in the budget formulation. Most significantly, it began to define the objectives and shape the policies of federal involvement in housing and in urban development. Priorities were better defined and programs reoriented, laying a basis for new instruments of policy that permitted reductions in expenditures with increased impact in a difficult economic environment.

Nevertheless, the public image of MSUA continued under a cloud. As the Government's leadership of federal-provincial relations became increasingly controversial, MSUA appeared more and more of a liability because it was a constant forum for attack. As the '70s came to an end, the Trudeau Government came to look upon MSUA first, as a front for a retreat to show the public federal sensitivity to provincial demands and, ultimately, as a piece of the government apparatus to sacrifice in order to demonstrate federal sensitivity to popular concern with "Big Government". As the 1979 general election came down upon it, the Trudeau Government declared victory and wound up the Ministry of State for Urban Affairs.

Experts in urban affairs will form their own view of whether or not

MSUA advanced the substance of their concerns. From my own perspective, it was wound up just as it was beginning to succeed. Even in the doubly disputed area of international relations with regard to urban development, it had towards the end seemed to reach a "modus vivendi" between federal, provincial and municipal authorities in Canada. The authority of its Minister and the credibility of its officials were established. The line between policy and operations had been defined. The expansionary imperative of its bureaucracy had been contained, yet in terms of policy innovation and research encouragement it was increasingly productive. Even in that most incendiary of political and bureaucratic quagmires, effectiveness measurement, it was breaking the ground which is essential to our really coming to grips with the problems of "Big Government".

More particularly, MSUA provided a voice for urban affairs at the national level within the government up to the highest levels. It provided a focus upon, and a forum for, national debate that is desperately needed if government is to be founded securely upon the levels closest to the people rather than to be gradually transferred further away from the people as has seemed the inexorable process exemplified by our organization for education and for local services. Certainly, MSUA achieved a definition of federal objectives,—and of the policies and programs for reaching those objectives,—coordination of decision-making and a testing of policy and program effectiveness, all within a constitutionally acceptable relationship to principles of ministerial and bureaucratic responsibility and accountability, that were very promising.

Whether in the case of MSUA or MSERD or MSSD, the real reason for their abandonments was not so much because of their failure to achieve their purposes. To the contrary, it lay in a desire to demonstrate a new attitude to economy in government on the part of the Trudeau Government and of its successors, a gut reaction to "Big Government" and a renewed freedom for individual Ministers and departments to have their own way.

But the complexity results from increased inter-dependence and growing technology. It will not go away. And the simple response of reducing the size of government, laudable as that is, and elusive as it has been in the hands of its keenest advocates, will not reduce its complexity even if it is ever achieved, which it certainly has not been so far,—whether in Great Britain, the United States or Canada. The brave new worlds of Messrs. Turner and Mulroney have led to Ministers and departments no more free. To the contrary, they have been characterized by a tendency for the right hand to know not what the left hand is doing, a proclivity to short term deal-making,—and increasingly in recent times, to "ad hoc-ery" and a lack of focus.

In this environment the natural inclination of every government is to centralize. In our system, it is for power to accumulate around the Prime Minister and for officials to function either out of fear of the Prime Minister or in an inchoate compact of power with him. In some ways,—order-in-council appointments outside of the traditional purview of the Prime Minister, for example,—we are seeing this process taking place in Ottawa today. It is an unhealthy development. It disturbs—damagingly, perhaps fatally—the equilibrium between the Prime Minister and his Ministers that is central to the interplay of responsibility and accountability in a Parliamentary system. It is the inevitable surrender to compelxity that Messrs. Pearson, Trudeau and Clark were so mindful to avoid.

It is increasingly clear that the ways to dealing with inter-dependence, technology and pro-activity that lie through evolution within the parameters of constitutional principle, all involve Parliamentary reform to increase the effectiveness of individual members and to provide more open government. These are, in the final analysis, the lynch-pins of any effective solution to our problems.

The Ministry of State mechanism is but one response along these lines. It has its defects, as all mechanisms will have, and no doubt there are other mechanisms that may be better. It was, in any event, only one of a number of reforms and, in a sense, it was always an experiment in evolution. Both MSERD and MSSD, for example, were explicitly conceived as possible routes to consolidations of micro-economic and social policy departments. MSUA might well have been folded into a broader response to the needs of federal-provincial coordination. The lesson of all the Government Organization Acts of the late '60s and early '70s was to know what you were doing before you did it and, in this regard, these Ministeries of State were seen as half-way houses to the information needed to complete the job.

Now these functions are buried deep in the bowels of departments, away almost as much from the busy Minister and, even, from his Deputy Minister, as from Ministers collectively. We are increasingly back to the pre-Pearson situation: either the functions are not being done or they are being done away from Ministers. In any case, Parliament and the public do not have access to them.

Inevitably, the cycle in Ottawa will turn—some suspect has begun already to turn—towards readdressing explictly decision-making in an increasingly inter-dependent and technological world. One hears from time to time the term "rational government", in a pejorative, deprecating, rather condescending tone, applied to such reforms of the '60s and '70s and '80s as the Minister of State system. It is as though government organization and process should not be rational.

It is a platitude,—but apparently bears re-stating,—that government reform must be a "rational" process. The result must be, and certainly can be, more efficient, effective and democratic decision-making. But to be so, the results must, again, be "rational". "Rational" in this situation means not only thought through, but constitutional.

The Ministry of State system is one of many means for organizing government decision-making to know what we are doing and to provide for accountability, within a Parliamentary government and to the public. Such decision-making must be many things in addition to being rational. But if it is not rational as well, what should it be? How otherwise are popular needs to be expressed? How considered? Above all, how otherwise is democracy to be preserved?

These are matters that go far beyond urban affairs. Yet, they also lie at the root of urban policy-making. Thus, when assessing how urban affairs should have been addressed in the past or judging how they should be addressed in the future,—as, indeed, when one considers any other activity of government,—concerns for rationality in organization and process must be a part of the judgement.

SECTION TWO

FEDERAL, PROVINCIAL AND MUNICIPAL PERSPECTIVES

THE MINISTRY OF STATE FOR URBAN AFFAIRS AND THE REGIONALIZATION OF FEDERAL URBAN PROGRAMS

Andre Saumier

Governments deal in facts and politicians deal in images and perceptions. The statisticians can thus construct a 2x2 matrix, and the political scientist will speculate on, and analyze, what happens when facts, images and perceptions converge or diverge, both at a given moment and over time. Since politicians are in power and exercise it, they can bend or even ignore facts to suit their perceptions. However, since facts are obdurate and must finally prevail, any **long lived** Ministry must submit to them. This is when government, and the civil servants who run it, finally come into their own. Public servants on the other hand are less concerned with perceptions and images. A sort of reverse gap can therefore emerge, and the Ministry itself can become estranged from the electorate, ultimately to be replaced by a new leadership. Whether that new leadership comes from within or without the ruling political party is in many ways irrelevant.

This abstruse introduction, while valid in its own right and worthy of careful pondering, is not altogether irrelevant to my assigned topic, as I shall try to demonstrate presently. The Urban Affairs Ministry might indeed be seen as an isolated and essentially accidental event, bursting comet—like on the bureaucratic sky in 1971 and vanishing in similar fashion five or six years later. It can, however, also be seen as child of its time and a specific eddy or mode in the fluctuating force fields of facts, perceptions and images as they obtained in the early 1970's. I must subscribe to that latter view, if only because I devoted some four years of hard and rewarding work to its creation, development and ultimate demise.

People may recall the last year of the Pearson Ministry; the triumph of the centennial and of Expo; the chill of De Gaulle's utterance from the Montreal City Hall Balcony; the twists and turns and constant sniping of Daniel Johnson; the Trudeau-Johnson debate, if it can be called that; the weakness at the center; the incessant bickering between powerful ministers each running his private fiefdom according to his own lights and ambitions. It was a bit like the Fronde in France except that the King was old rather than a child. Mr. Pearson's announcement that he would step down as leader of the Liberal Party precipitated a predictable event: the Ministry almost ceased to exist as an entity capable of shaping events and of asserting the federal role in a cohesive, effective and persuasive fashion. In brief, there was a growing weakness at the center and a proliferation of absurd skirmishes at the periphery.

It was to be Trudeau's task, which he embraced most eagerly, to remedy that perilous situation: strengthen the center; cow the proud barons of the Ministry; despatch trusted lieutenants to the marches of the imperium and bring the local warlords to their knees; gather into his hands the cracked pieces of federal power; reshape them into structured thrusts, and hurl them into battle. But what battle? I contend that it was a battle for federal power, for French power, for federal initiative, for logic and design to prevail.

The potential fields of battle, whether theoretical or real, were many. They were surveyed quickly and armies sent forth, while Athens-on-the-Rideau flourished under its philosopher king. As Victor Hugo puts it in Ruy Blas: ''Il sera Richelieu, s'il n'est Olivares''.

In this frenzy of activity, much of which was on paper and comparable to the studies of the German general staff between the two wars, several things became apparent and a source of growing intellectual frustration.

First, the traditional departments were like the Macedonian Phalanx: irresistible when finally on the move, but ponderous and mindless. Second, the political map that had presided over their design was quickly being superseded by events and, in many instances, was no longer relevant: what federal department, for example, could address the problems of cities? The answer was simple: none. Yet, Canada's population was increasingly urban and the federal government useless and, worse still, invisible to them. Third, existing departments, while dimwitted and archaic, had entrenched territorial claims which were difficult to challenge. Nor was it easy to reshuffle their constituent parts into punchier, more aggressive organizations. Fourth, what was really needed was not massive bodies of programs overwhelming all resistance, but small, commando like, Panzer-type bodies that could form and reform quickly and use whatever weapons the traditional armies contained and that could get around various Maginot lines. For there were Maginot lines guarding the promising lands Ottawa wanted to and needed to invest in, in its quest for relevance to the new situations that it perceived.

This is my fifth point: the Maginot lines were the traditional areas of provincial jurisdiction. These areas—education, municipal affairs, land, leisure, culture, etc—did not appear very promising to the Fathers of Confederation when they were meeting, so they were left to the Provinces, while they kept railroads, ports, wharves and canals. Yet, the times they are a-changing, as Dylan wrote, and the really exciting things were behind these obsolete, irrelevant, counter productive but impregnable Maginot lines which were well guarded by jumpy provincial politicians always awake and ready to blow their loud bugle at the slightest nocturnal noise. The story of the Department of Manpower and Immigration and of its Adult Education Program, bogged down for years at, and despite great expense, in front of these Maginot lines, had not been lost on anyone.

A subtle and creative mind, who shall remain nameless, saw a way around these difficulties which, like all brilliant strokes, was at once simple and disarming: Ministries of State. They would be light organizations created by order-in-council under a vgeneral enabling law, easily put together and easily dismantled, without programs— hence not threatening anyone either in Ottawa or provincially—but with strong coordinating mandates—hence to be reckoned with—and considerable research funds—hence strong intellectual leadership and big brains. In a way, all brain and no brawn.

These Ministries were given the job of succeeding where all others had failed. The concept was greeted with a contemptuous and very brief snort by the entrenched bureaucratic barons. As for the provinces, their deepest suspicions were immediately aroused and they quickly reached the conclusion, at least in the case of Urban Affairs, that here was a most devious and dangerous Trojan horse. Instantly dismissed as negligible by the Federal Departments whose programs they were supposed to reshape and deploy—without however paying for them— and immediately, declared **persona non grata** by the Provinces, and forbidden any contact with their municipalities, the emissaries of the Ministry of State for Urban Affairs started to work.

As I travel today across the country, I look with a sense of pride and accomplishment at several interesting sights:

- — The Waterfront Development in Halifax
- — the Civic Centre and City Square in Saint-John, Newfoundland
- — the Vieux-Port in Montreal
- — the Vieux-Port in Quebec City
- — the Harbourfront in Toronto
- — the absence of an international airport in Pickering
- — the Trizec complex in Winnipeg
- — the Rideau Canal Waterway in Ontario
- — Granville Island in Vancouver
- — the Lachine Canal re-development in Quebec
- — the railroad relocation projects in Regina

The above is an incomplete list of concrete projects studied, proposed and shepherded by the Coordination Branch of the Urban Affairs Ministry. They have several features in common. They were all discarded, initially, as either stupid or unrealistic or both; all were more or less forced upon reluctant Ottawa Departments by unholy, ramshackle and ad hoc alliances of local and provincial politicians and public servants using the Ministry's senior officers as partners in intrigue through so-called tri-partite committees; all called upon a variety of federal programs but the seed money for research and initial concepts came from the Ministry; none was actually implemented by the Ministry itself; all were opportunistic in nature, resulting from careful analysis of available opportunities and levers, but within a rigorous general framework; all required months and in some cases years of frustrating patient negotiations; none were really foisted by brute force upon unwilling provincial or municipal partners, despite acknowledged and often purposely engineered rhetoric to the contrary; for one project that succeeded, five were stillborn or abandoned in mid-course.

So, in the event, small did prove beautiful and apparent weakness proved to be a source of strength.

It may be useful to expand somewhat on the conceptual and tactical framework that was used during those exciting years.

The conceptual framework was provided in essence by Professor Harvey Lithwick in his series of monographs on Urban Canada for the late Robert Andras, who was then Minister responsible for CMHC and who became the first Minister of State for Urban Affairs. Lithwick showed that a vast array of federal programs impacted powerfully on

Canadian cities but in accidental if not indeed unintentional, blind or even contradictory and counterproductive fashion. He showed furthermore that the Federal government was a most significant urban land holder, but that the full extent of these holdings was in fact unknown—and I doubt whether it is known to this day—while the holdings themselves were put to haphazard uses when they were put to any use at all. He showed several amusing instances where one Federal Department was busy acquiring land at great expense while another had land lying idle nearby or was busy selling it for a pittance. He showed also that the situation was compounded exponentially if one took Crown Corporations into account. He argued forcefully that Urban Canada was, so to speak, where the action was and that Ottawa was therefore derelict in its duties vis-a-vis the citizens of this country if it did not put its urban act together in some minimal fashion.

Lithwick then went on to propose two more things.

The first was an administrative model to deal with the Urban problem. He recommended a Federal Department of Urban Affairs on—to me at least—the most traditional Departmental model, which would agglomerate all the significant existing federal "urban programs" and ride herd on other Departments as far as their "urban" activities were concerned. That was a naive suggestion, unworkable in theory and practice, which was ultimately, and fortunately, discarded.

The second was the first cut of a conceptual model of urban Canada accompanied by population forecasts for our major urban centers. This led to the formulation of an "urban policy field" as a valid focus for further theoretical, applied and policy research. Considerable human and financial resources were devoted by the Ministry to the validation and development of that field leading to significant research outputs and culminating in massive and, on the whole, fairly arcane draft submissions to Cabinet. An interesting side-product was the attempt to develop a computerized urban model, integrating current and forecasted urban populations. The last Cabinet Memorandum with which I was associated, and indeed wrote in substantial parts, tried to bring together all these threads into a proposed "Federal Urban Policy" with consequent programs. That memorandum I believe was shipwrecked in the turmoil that accompanied the attempted integration of CMHC, the National Capital Commission and the Ministry in late 1975. In any event, it now strikes me in retrospect as a pretty far-out document with too little connection either with governmental structure or with the perceptions and images of the politicians of the time. The Urban scenario which was presented was called the "unconstrained growth scenario" if I recall correctly, and had in it some rather scary population forecasts which, fortunately, did not come to pass. I believe it a tribute to the common-sense wisdom of politicians that they were not taken in by these forecasts despite the sophisticated mumbo-jumbo with which they were put forward.

In any event, it did seem to me at the time that Lithwick had hit pay dirt with his federal urban lands analysis and that here was at least one effective lever available to the fledgling Ministry.

The tactics followed quite logically. We spread the word around the country that Ottawa had significant reservoirs of both poorly used and unused urban lands that could be put to good or better purpose if we could only sit together provincially and municipally and agree on it. I lived for many months in fear and trepidation lest someone really took us up on this offer, for a very simple reason. These federal lands were by and large in the hands of Public Works and National Defense. I had reason to believe that neither of these two well established Departments would see the wisdom of parting with their real estate at the behest of this upstart Ministry, and for purposes far removed from their own concerns, if not inimical to them. In that I was not proven wrong. I did approach Sylvain Cloutier, at one time, with a proposal to re-cycle an essentially unused but strategically located armory in a downtown area. Sylvain informed me that he saw the wisdom of that scheme; unfortunately he added, that armory is likely to play a pivotal role in the emerging Canadian Defense Strategy—a topic he could not enlarge upon because I did not enjoy the required high-level security clearance— and hence had to be retained by DND for the foreseeable future. I came to the conclusion after a second attempt, that the emerging Defense Strategy was likely to encompass, as far as the Ministry was concerned, all DND urban holdings however minute and unknown to the Department itself, and gave up on that one.

At Public Works, John MacDonald was quick to see the rationale behind my arguments. He immediately put together a group of his own with the mandate of forming a Federal Lands Policy to be administered by his Department. I had foreseen this however, and confident that the inner wheels of DPW would, as was their wont, grind very slowly, I put together a joint Ministry—CMHC, submission to Treasury Boad on the very same issue (no mean accomplishment I may add.) While that submission was worming its way through the Treasury Board gauntlet, I was informed by my Senior Coordinator for the Atlantic Provinces that a good friend of his in another Federal Department had told him that Public Works was about to realize its long held dream of erecting a new federal building in Halifax, that the land had been selected and was about to be purchased, and that the proposed location was, in his friend's view at least, both intrinsically poor and potentially controversial. That struck me as a very pregnant situation. Contacts in the office of the Premier of Nova Scotia informed me that some of the most senior personal staff of the Premier were not keen on the proposed location, although not opposed to the building itself which in their view was long overdue. I was further informed that it would be easy for the Premier's office to stir up opposition by City Hall to the DPW proposal and that the proposal could therefore be stymied for a brief period of time. Since, however, both the Province and the City were bent upon a new federal building, they would all fall quickly behind the DPW proposal if the alternative was a further postponement. Add to this the intelligence that this building was the pet project of the DPW Regional Director, who had labored on it for years and was most determined to see the first ground turned before his shortly to be announced scheduled retirement.

Faced on the one hand with my Treasury Board Submission, which by then had found favour with the Assistant Secretary—programs of the Board—and to which the Secretary himself was said not to be opposed—and confronted with some unanticipated local static to its plans on the other hand, DPW agreed to consider our analysis of the pros and cons of their proposed site. Our analysis was of course dismissed out of hand by DPW when it was produced. In the meantime, however, I had been able to set up a Federal—Provincial—Municipal Committee in Halifax, with some powerful provincial elements chairing it. That Committee then decided that the proposed Federal Building was a key developmental infrastructure from an urban point of view. It was therefore within its self-appointed mandate to examine it critically before a final choice was made. That view as well as the existence of this new Committee did not sit well with DPW, to say the least. But they had been cut off at the pass, so to speak, and had to accept a further review. While the Committee, which by definition could not meet immediately, deliberated, a tiny urban design group I had secretly formed within the Ministry, assisted by some local consultants, suggested by the Province, studied the situation and came up with a view that the Federal Building could be used to revitalize the Halifax Waterfront, which was by then in a state of terminal decay, and that it should be located there on lands which belonged to the Province.

That recommendation was endorsed by the Committee and forwarded by it, along with some preliminary designs, to DPW, where it received a somewhat lukewarm response. I could carry on like this for a long time. Suffice it to say, that the Federal Building now sits on the waterfront, that it is part of a very interesting group of buildings and is remarkable in many respects.

This is how my Branch of the Ministry operated on a daily basis. It was, on the whole, fairly successful. We did not achieve nor did we try to, a complete or even partial integration of Federal urban programs. Such an attempt was neither feasible nor desirable. Indeed, the Ministry finally came to an end when it did try to create a slightly more unified focus of some federal urban programs by joining it organizationally with CMHC and the NCC. That was too much of a threat to the established order of things and was bound to fail, as it did.

Nor would I recommend that a new Ministry of Urban Affairs be created. The Ministry was a child of a particular time, which has passed. Planning is now out of fashion, urban design is out of fashion, citizen groups are out of fashion, government intervention itself is out of fashion. The facts are now different, while the images and perceptions have themselves changed. I would like to end my remarks by quoting someone who said: ''The universe unfolds as it should?''

RECOLLECTIONS FROM A PROVINCIAL PERSPECTIVE

Victor C. Goldbloom

Taking a public trip down memory lane is not without its dangers. There are two in particular which I would like to recognize at this point of departure.

One is encapsulated in the well-known French expression, "La Memoire est la faculte qui oublie"—memory is the faculty which forgets. The other is of a more personal nature: I am obliged to relive a time of discomfort and even of anger, a time of frustrations which were often focussed on what we perceived as a lack of constructive progress.

Intergovernmental relations, being expressions of government policies and positions, must be largely independent of interpersonal relations. Having said that, let me immediately also say that my personal relations with my successive Federal counterparts were, and have remained, extremely good. There were, of course, differences in personality and approach. The chronology of my own involvement was such that I had only a rather brief relationship with Bob Andras; but in these few contacts I found him warm, sensitive, open and imaginative. Ron Basford, who today is a good friend and a valued member of the board of the organization which I have the honour to head, the Canadian Council of Christians and Jews, was no less friendly and open but was a tougher negotiator, at least in style. Barney Danson, a different personality again, was the one I knew best; actually, I had not known him before, but he had an enthusiasm for Federal-Provincial Conferences which his predecessors had not had, and so we found ourselves in Ottawa several times a year for animated discussions. The person I had known for a very long time was the Deputy Minister, Peter Oberlander.

One thing was always clear and never at issue: we were, on each side, concerned Canadians, sincerely trying to conciliate differing points of

50

view. We were, to each other, a stimulating and even an enjoyable intellectual challenge.[1]

I indicated that we met often, Federal and provincial ministers; and I indicated also that we nevertheless fell short of achieving significant agreement. Let me point out that some of these Federal-Provincial Conferences brought together Ministers of Municipal Affairs, some Ministers of Housing and some Ministers of the Environment, and that the individuals were not necessarily the same. If my memory serves me correctly, I was one of the relatively few people who were Ministers of both Municipal Affairs and Housing, and generally the only one who was Minister of the Environment as well.

These variations in responsibilities sometimes complicated discussions, as for example when the subject was the treatment of municipal sewage. I remarked at the outset of frustration in the absence of constructive progress, and this is a pertinent example, especially for a pragmatist who basically believes that it is results that count. A formula for financial assistance existed, and the Federal contribution within it was proportionally small, the larger portion being left to the province and its municipalities. Quebec offered to bear a significant percentage of that larger portion, but there were essentially no takers. We pressed for an increase in the Federal share, but without success; the argument was that in other provinces, particularly Ontario, many municipalities had installed sewage treatment plants under the existing financing formula, and that it would be unfair to them if the formula were subsequently made more generous; but the result was that the sewage continued untreated.

Another area of frustrating disagreement and lack of achievement was in the housing field. Federal programs of financial assistance were designed to encourage home ownership, an objective with which it is hard to take issue. The design of those programs, however, seemed to favour the single-family dwelling with a plot of land around it—and the cost of providing water supply, sewage lines, police protection and garbage disposal was in general inversely proportional to the housing density. We pressed for formula modifications which would encourage higher and therefore more economical densities, citing studies and projects which achieved medium density while providing good values in air, light, privacy and green space, as well as recreational facilities and relative security, but although we achieved some understanding we did not achieve as much movement as we would have liked.

One of our most frustrating experiences was the battle for block funding, spearheaded by Ontario and Alberta. (Quebec, with its particular perspective of Federal-Provincial relations, was generally happy if it did not always have to be the principal spokesperson of provincial disagreement with the Federal government.) The provinces argued that where a field of responsibility was clearly, constitutionally in the provincial domain, it was only fair that the Federal government should make its contribution as a lump sum and allow the provinces to determine the priorities for its use, always of course within the specific field to which the money was assigned. Housing, in this instance, was the case in point. It was particularly frustrating to hear the Prime Minister say, on more than one occasion, "Maybe the provinces have their priorities wrong . . . "—especially since the government of which I was a part had created a Cabinet committee on land use planning and management which met regularly, discussed intensely, produced thoughtful conclusions and had as its secretary Andre Saumier.

This brings me, then, to a consideration of the tri-level process, and of our general refusal to participate in it. It was in many respects a Hobson's choice: we were very much preoccupied with the old French dictum that "les absents ont toujours tort"—which literally means that those who are absent are always in the wrong and carries the sense that those who are absent abdicate their share in the decision-making process. I do recall, however, attending one tri-level encounter at which an emergency meeting of provincial ministers was called at about five o'clock one afternoon because it had come to light that the municipalities had had a meeting with the Federal representatives in our absence. We did not, as I remember, go again; nor did I attend any of the conventions of the Canadian Federation of Mayors and Municipalities.

It was, and I say this in all sincerity, painful for me to refuse. I had particularly good relationships with virtually all the mayors and municipal councillors in the province, and I never missed a convention of the Union of Municipalities or the Union of County Councils. I was sensitive also to the slightly demeaning definition of municipalities as "creatures" of the provinces; and I could understand the municipalities' financial constraints and the limitations and possible unfairness of the property tax base. It was, however, a matter of deeply-held and indeed constitutional principle.

The government of which I was a part took the position that since municipal affairs were constitutionally in the provincial domain, conferences involving the Federal government should in fact be bi-level, with municipal representation forming a part of the provincial delegation and any provincial-municipal disagreements being worked out in advance. The municipalities were reluctant to accept this arrangement, and the Federal government, interested in being politically significant in the municipal field, gave it no support. I could understand the viewpoints and objectives; I could understand the readiness of the municipalities to become the clientele of the equally ready Ministry of State for Urban Affairs; but I could not agree or acquiesce.

On two occasions in the later '70s, a public opinion survey was done in Quebec, and both gave the identical, fascinating results. Respondents were given a list of governmental responsibilities—agriculture, defence, education, transport, etc.—and were asked to indicate which they thought should be Federal, which provincial and which shared. When the answers were compiled, they added up, in clear majority, to the constitution we have today.

Since we were living at that time through an intense period of discussion about the presumed dissatisfaction of Quebec's population with the existing federal system, the interpretation of these results was, to say the least, perplexing. My colleague and close friend Raymond Garneau felt that if the problem was not in the constitution, it had to be in the country's major federal institutions: the Senate, the Supreme Court, etc. This was one of the rare occasions on which I disagreed with him. I felt, and feel, that the essential problem is that whereas the constitution defines in principle who does what, in practice that definition is not adequately respected—the debate on block funding, to which I referred before, is a pertinent example. In fields of provincial jurisdiction such as housing and certain municipal affairs, the Federal government, with its dominant taxing and spending powers, will establish criteria and priorities, pre-empting the provincial domain. The Federal argument is that the money it distributes has been raised from all Canadian taxpayers, and that the Federal government has therefore the right and indeed the obligation to ensure that it is spent wisely. I find that argument—forgive my bluntness—insulting to duly elected, equally responsible provincial governments; and I also submit that it fails to recognize the reality of different priorities in different parts of the country.

Notwithstanding these negative observations, it was predominantly enjoyable and intellectually exhilarating to work with the Ministry of State for Urban Affairs. The failure to resolve the disagreements I have outlined was, notwithstanding our reciprocal goodwill, our common failure; and it must remain our common regret.

NOTES

1. I shall always be deeply grateful to the Federal Government of the day and to Ron Basford in particular, for having designated me one of Canada's six delegates to the United Nations Conference on the Environment at Stockholm in 1972, and again as one of Canada's nine delegates to the United Nations Habitat Conference on Human Settlements at Vancouver in 1976 where I was Second Vice-Chairman of the Canadian delegation.

THE GOLDEN HOUR OF MUNICIPAL POLITICS

D. G. NEWMAN

When I received an invitation to participate in ''The Canadian Urban Experience—Past and Present'' Conference at the University of Winnipeg in August 1985, I was delighted to have the opportunity to meet again some extraordinary Canadians who, in the 1960's and early '70s, worked exceedingly hard on a process designed to put in place a mechanism to deal with the growing urbanization of Canada.

The process was tri-level in nature, Federal, Provincial and Municipal, and the mechanism was the Annual Tri-level Conference.

The Federal Government had constructed the Ministry of State for Urban Affairs. The Provinces had a variety of ministries from Minister of Urban Affairs through Minister of Municipal Affairs, and Minister of Community Affairs to Minister of Intergovernmental Affairs, all speaking to the issue of urbanization. The Municipalities had the Canadian Federation of Mayors and Municipalities at the national level and some 18 Associations of Municipalities at the Provincial level representing urban and rural Municipalities and Metropolitan, County and Regional governments.

The Municipalities believed that the Annual Tri-level Conference was an integral part of the mechanism necessary to deal with the process of urbanization in Canada. Without it, we would invariably arrive at inappropriate solutions where priorities were skewered, investments put into disrepute, and distortions created in programs painstakingly constructed by one or other level of government.

But perhaps the most exciting political result was the dawning of the golden hour of municipal politics in Canada. There followed also a serious maturing of the Provincial Government System through an increased awareness of their constitutional position in the Canadian federation.

The golden hour of municipal politics began with the rather coura-geous action of the Government of Ontario in putting into place the Municipality of Metropolitan Toronto in 1958.

It was an attempt to provide a sufficient mechanism to deal with the question of the urbanization of the Greater Toronto area. What followed the formation of Metro Toronto, however, was exceedingly important.

This was a period of intensive urban and regional planning in Ontario, which ultimately lead to the formation of regional government through much of Southern Ontario. I believe this had a dramatic effect on the form and functioning of municipal government in much of the rest of Canada. Quebec introduced its comprehensive regional plan; B.C. as well; P.E.I. regionalized the educational system; New Brunswick intervened in the rural areas and effectively took over their manage-ment; Winnipeg got Unicity, and so on.

But, there was another significant result. Municipalities were grad-ually beginning to understand the meaning and use of power. As the systems grew larger, in response to need, and the staffs more sophisti-cated, and the politicians more informed, municipal government was maturing.

At the National Municipal level, under the aegis of the Canadian Federation of Mayors and Municipalities, a group was gathering, particularly from the cities and principal towns of Canada. They included people like Ab Campbell from Metro Toronto, Ivor Dent from Edmonton, Allan O'Brien from Halifax, Giles Lamontagne from Quebec City, to mention only a few. Generally, they were people with a more expansive point of view, who saw the need for larger systems and better staff to respond to the needs of the turbulent '60s; people who had, in more cases, come through the municipal associations in their respective Provinces, and were now acting at the national level.

And they were beginning to talk in serious terms about equating responsibility with authority and resources to meet their responsibili-ties. Municipal expenditures were getting close to 30 percent of total government expenditures reflecting their enlarging responsibility to not only deliver their own services, but to be the community deliverer of Federal and Provincial programs. At the same time, they saw them-selves as having little real authority to adjust the programs to address serious social issues that surfaced in their communities.

In most of Canada, Municipalities had access only to property tax as a source of unconditional revenue. As their expenditure responsibilities increased, they became increasingly dependant on Provincial funding for extra revenue which came with conditions attached, reflecting Provincial priorities. That was the state of things municipal when I joined the National Board of Directors of the Federation, some time after my election as the Mayor of Whitby in 1966.

During the next 10 years, municipal government in Canada would rise to its greatest height politically at the First National Tri-level Conference in Toronto in November 1972, and would fall back into a more subservient statutory role under intense Provincial pressure right across the country. The way would be cleared for what is now history—the consummation of the Constitutional Accords, the division of powers between federal and provincial governments, and the patriation of the Canadian Constitution—almost without a word from Canada's municipal government.

How then was that previous moment of greatness achieved? As always, of course, with an enormous amount of work by a few dedicated souls, at all three levels.

Let me turn your attention for a moment back to the 1960s and the regional planning process which was in place in Ontario and elsewhere. It was causing municipal politicians to think in terms of consensus and response to these provincial initiatives. In Ontario, where there were three municipal organizations, we established a committee called the MLC (Municipal Liaison Committee), which consisted of the executive members of the three associations. This was the organization which responded to Premier John Robarts' call for a Provincial-Municipal conference in Ontario in 1970. That was less than a year after Mr. Trudeau raised the question of a constitutional role for municipal government in Canada in addressing the Federation's Annual Meeting in Ottawa in June 1969. A year later, Bob Andras, in addressing the Federation's Annual Meeting in Halifax, talked about the formation of a National Urban Council.

1970 was also the year that the Ministers of Municipal Affairs, meeting in August in Winnipeg under the chairmanship of Mr. Howard Pawley, then Minister of Municipal Affairs of Manitoba, received a deputation from a joint municipal committee of the Federation and several Provincial Associations of Municpalities, to formally begin the process which led to the First National Tri-level Conference.

I emphasize that it was a joint municipal committee because we had a serious problem to contend with on the municipal side. Of the 18 municipal associations across the country, five associations did not recognize the Federation as the national spokesman for municipal government, and the only way we could bring them into the fold was to establish something called the JMCIR—the Joint Municipal Committee on Intergovernmental Relations—consisting of the Federation with representation for the other entities. The Chairman was Mayor Allan O'Brien of Halifax, the past president of the Federation. It would later be agreed, however, that the current president of the Federation would become the Chairman of the JMCIR.

But the whole arrangement was a symptom of division. At the time it was dreadful; later on it became a symbol of victory and, in fact, became our finest hour.

Returning for the moment to the meeting with the Ministers, we filed a document called "The Municipality of the Canadian Federation". That document was the heart and soul of the municipal plea for recognition and it became our base document. We had worked on it for over a year with Dr. Eric Reecroft from the University of Western Ontario. The document was intended to put into perspective the work being done by municipal government, and the critical significance of that work in the overall system of government in Canada. It talked about the reality of that responsibility in the light of inadequate municipal authority and resources and the subordination of its own interest and desires to apparently insensitive decrees from the federal and provincial governments. It addressed its de facto position as a level of government, and started the process of gently making the case for a de jure position as the third level of government in Canada. Above all, it was an urgent plea for cooperation among the three levels of government to solve the problems of urbanization as they were being reflected in both the urban and rural landscapes.

The impact of the document can be best summed up in the following extract from a confidential assessment of the meeting by one of our staff members:

Anyone with high expectations of the immediate achievement of the objective as stated in the position paper might have come away from the meeting of August 18th, with the Provincial Ministers of Municipal Affairs, with a sense of frustration and disappointment.

There seemed to be a lack of understanding on the part of some of the Ministers for the real thrust of the Federation's argument.

One might be pardoned for wondering just how thoroughly the paper had been examined and analyzed in certain instances. Perhaps the case would have been more clearly put had a brief precis been included with the presentation at the meeting, although that should surely not have been necessary.

That was the beginning of a long and hazardous process involving many meetings at every level. It culminated with a directive from the meeting of First Ministers in August of 1972 in Halifax, that the First National Tri-level Conference be held in Toronto under the direction of the three co-chairmen—Mr. Basford, representing the Federal Government, Mr. Mooney of Nova Scotia, representing the Provinces, and myself as President of the Federation, representing the Municipalities.

We were ecstatic. We worked continuously for three months, developed our position, sought and received endorsement from the 18 Provincial Associations, translated and bound the documents and deposited them with Henry Davis, Secretary of the Constitutional Secretariat, one week before the Conference. The municipal position was comprehensive. It had gradually been evolving for some three years. The submission was in three parts. The first paper was entitled the "Canadian Community". It was an overview of the current socio-economic-political environment in Canada. It was an attempt to identify the problems and challenges that governments faced in their public responsibilities and to relate them to the special roles which each jurisdiction currently played. The second paper was much more specific and dealt with the following subjects: transportation, housing, environmental management, leisure and recreation, and public assistance. The third paper entitled "Policies, Programs and Finance" was directed to the design and development of means to find solutions through the machinery of intergovernmental consultation and cooperation and tax redistribution.

The Federal Government did their thing. The Provinces did not. Let me add a few names for the record at this time. The two Federal Ministers of State for Urban Affairs, who were deeply involved in the process, were Bob Andras and Ron Basford. The three Provincial Ministers of Municipal Affairs, who chaired the Annual Meetings of the Ministers, were (1970) Howard Pawley, Manitoba, (1971) Don Campbell, B.C. and (1972) Fraser Mooney, Nova Scotia. The four Mayors, who held the office of President of the Federation, were (1969) Al O'Brien, Halifax, (1970) Ivor Dent, Edmonton, Alberta, (1971) Marcel D'Armour, Hull, Quebec, and (1972) myself, Des Newman from Whitby, Ontario. It happened, however, that during D'Armour's year as President of the Federation, he was kept at home on several occasions because of municipal business and I substituted for him on the joint Federal-Provincial-Municipal Chairmen's Committee. As a result, when my term as President arrived, and I joined Basford and Mooney on the Chairmen's Committee, I had already had a year of on-the-job training.

Now to the Conference itself. We arrived on site Sunday, 19 November 1972, at the newly constructed Sheraton Centre for that historic meeting. I would now like to recount, in a very personal way, the story which made my entire public life worthwhile.

I mentioned earlier that five associations were not members of the Federation per se, when the process began. They were all rural associations from Ontario, Quebec, Manitoba, Alberta and Saskatchewan. They participated from the beginning—but they always carefully retained a position outside the Federation. They did so in order to maintain what they considered to be their very special access to their Provincial Governments, and they saw their distancing themselves from the Federation as their oath of allegiance to their Provincial masters. However, once the word was given by the First Ministers, Ontario and Quebec joined the Federation. That left Manitoba, Alberta and Saskatchewan. About one month later, Abe Yanofsky invited me to speak to the Manitoba Association of Urban Municipalities. At that meeting was the President of the Union of Manitoba Municipalities, which represented the essentially rural municipalities.

The case which I put to the association and its executive was a simple one. If the rural municipalities did not join the urban municipalities at this time and support the thrust for greater authority and resources, they would find it increasingly difficult to hold onto their farms as the labour drain continued from farm to city. They understood the impact that it would have in greater capitalization to replace men with machines, and the increased debt load that it would represent. Sufficient to say that, after that meeting, Manitoba joined the Federation. That left Alberta and Saskatchewan.

During the first day of the Conference, the Municipal Speakers, I believe, discharged their responsibilities well. The Federal Government produced carefully prepared papers in an attempt to assist the municipalities on one hand, without irritating the Provinces on the other. The Provinces, however, were in considerable disarray. They tabled a joint

Provincial paper and, no sooner had it hit the table, than Manitoba disclaimed any association with it. This broke the discipline, and all Provinces started hedging their bets. The Sessions Chairman, Senator Goldenburg, managed, however, to hold it all together rather well, and the day ended on a high note for the Municipalities.

The next morning, the 85 municipal delegates caucussed at a breakfast session prior to the start of the formal day's proceeding. During the course of that caucus, Reeve Evrett Murphy, President of Saskatchewan Association of Rural Municipalities, addressed the group. I will never forget his words:

"Mr. President, I wish to advise you that after yesterday's proceedings, Saskatchewan Rural Executive caucussed and has decided to join the Federation."

The room broke into bedlam. I looked at my watch. It was 8:25 A.M. on Tuesday, November 21, 1972. It was the moment which a lot of people had given many years of their lives for. For the first time in Canadian history, we could truly say that we had a National Municipal Concensus. One half hour later, during the opening remarks by the co-chairmen, I made the announcement that from that moment on, the Federation represented all of Municipal Government in Canada.

This announcement threw the Provinces into an uproar. The Hon. Mr. Woods, Minister of Municipal Affairs, initially would not believe the announcement. He was certain that the linkages which previously existed with the Rural Municipal Association, could not be broken. Indeed, the Sessions Chairman had to recess the session to allow the Provinces to regroup.

I would like to respond to one of the reasons often given for the start of the demise of the MSUA: that Quebec did not attend the Second Tri-level Conference which took place a year later in Edmonton. What really happened, beginning with the Second Tri-level Conference, was that the Provinces gradually started dismantling the process. They were assisted in this by the Municipalities, either through fear of reprisals or lack of leadership. The Provinces also recognized the unresolved and continuing conflict between MSUA and CMHC. In effect, the linkages between CMHC and the Provinces had been honed over a long period of time and were well understood, whereas the actions of MSUA were not only new and innovative but darkly questioned.

What of the future? I hold with that body of opinion which believes that urban social problems are being stored up, both in the U.S. and Canada, as we seek economic goals. One can observe, for example, the current attempts in both countries, to reduce the future costs of social services. I believe, however, that Mr. Reagan's successor will inherit those problems. I leave it to others to decide whether we can cease to be vigilant in protecting those who increasingly may not be able to protect themselves. I suppose it rests on the kind of society that we want to build.

It was the building of the caring society that first drew me into politics. As I progressed and learned and understood, more and more, the needs of this large stretched-out country, with its regional beauty, its regional resources, and its regional cultures, I began to appreciate more the need for its three levels of government. Clearly, each must have access to a share of the resources available, consistent with its share of the responsibilities. Clearly, constitutional definition to provide each with a charter of rights and responsibilities is needed. Such things, however, are not beyond human design or undertaking. The mechanisms of the Annual Tri-level Conference and MSUA were simply building blocks along the way. That neither survived was not an indication of need, but an indictment of the users. Indeed, the problems that prompted their genesis have not gone away. We have simply deferred their solution. We have thrown money at them, and papered them over with debt. Rather than recognizing the inability of the Federal and Provincial Governments to find solutions at the level of the community, we continue to pile bureaucracy onto bureaucracy rather than relinquish control to the municipality. The result is that they, like spoiled children, exhibit in the main little sense of a broader social responsibility, and the circle is complete.

My commitment to the equitable distribution of responsibility and resources between the three levels of government in this country remains unabated. The mechanisms which both Federal and Municipal Governments attempted to put in place are still valid, I commend to you, therefore, a small phrase taken from the ancient oath which the youth of Greece took on the occasion of their maturity:

. . . let us pass on our city not only not less but greater and more beautiful than it was passed to us.

SECTION THREE

ASSESSMENT AND REVIEW

URBAN IMPACT ASSESSMENT AND MSUA

Barry Wellar

This paper presents the rationale and scope of the concept of urban impact assessment (UIA). It then examines the policy formation and policy research records of the Ministry of State for Urban Affairs from that perspective.[1] The framework used to examine the UIA presence at MSUA is comprised of two models; an urban policy formation model, and a decision support system model. By means of a "content analysis" of hundreds of MSUA-related and MSUA-generated documents, it is demonstrated that in both principle and practice, UIA at MSUA, like MSUA itself, was a guiding light that flickered and burned brightly, and dimmed, and flickered, and . . .

Indications are that impact assessment—urban and otherwise[2]—is assuming increasing importance and acceptance because of growing recognition that the costs of errors in our urbanized society are becoming cumulative, compound, and in some cases extremely dangerous.[3] Perhaps one of the Ministry's more lasting, albeit "ex poste" contributions, could be to confirm and elaborate what was learned about impact assessment in conceptual and operational terms during the MSUA "experiment", and in particular the need to have an abiding concern about the *significance of consequences* of initiatives.[4].

Urban Impact Assessment

Urban Impact Assessment (UIA) is concerned, in general, with assessing or judging the significance of "urban" consequences or influences arising from policy formation and policy research initiatives.[5]

As suggested in Figure 1, impact assessment is regarded here as one class of inquiry, and is accorded the highest order in the (rudimentary) Decision Support System (DSS) model. That is, IA subsumes all the other classes of inquiry and their associated study inputs, throughputs and outputs in order to deal explicitly with *the* question that is not traditionally associated, in principle and practice, with the other classes: What is the *significance* (to society) of the consequence(s) arising from a policy or program initiative (of lack thereof)?

As observed by McLuhan (1962, p. 243), ". . . unconsciousness of the effect of any force is a disaster, especially a force that we have made ourselves".

The "urban force" is a force that we have made ourselves, and it was a pervasive reality in Canada prior to and during the Ministry's life. To paraphrase McLuhan, those responsible for precipitating or modifying the urban force should assess the societal significance of the intended or unintended consequences of their actions. Following McLuhan's exhortation, this paper uses an impact assessment perspective to review and examine the Ministry's concern with the impact(s) and effect(s) of the urban force.

UIA IN A DECISION SUPPORT SYSTEM (DSS) CONTEXT

The model presented *is* rudimentary, and open-ended. Boxes and entries can be modified to make the model as simple or as complex as readers might wish; what is shown is sufficient for the present paper.

Second, Dimensions A and B are inter-dependent in the policy formation and policy research domains.

Third, the dashed lines between the Dimensions are significant in two respects: every part of A does not necessarily relate to every part of B; and, the relationships between the Dimensions tend to be more of a likely or implied than a known or confirmed nature in many situations.

Fourth, regarding Dimension A, the Desired Outcome in a DSS Context is generally regarded to be "Effective Decision-Making" as it relates to policies and programs from inception through to implementation, monitoring and adjustment. The model has been modified, however, to reflect the present concern with a UIA perspective. Hence the Desired Outcome includes the additional reference to "Sound Judgements about the Significance of Urban Impacts/Effects of Policies and Programs".

And, fifth, regarding Dimension B, the Existing to Preferred States of Affairs relationships warrant a brief reference in terms of their normative/incremental implications.

FIGURE 1. RUDIMENTS OF A DECISION SUPPORT SYSTEM (DSS): FOR URBAN IMPACT ASSESSMENT

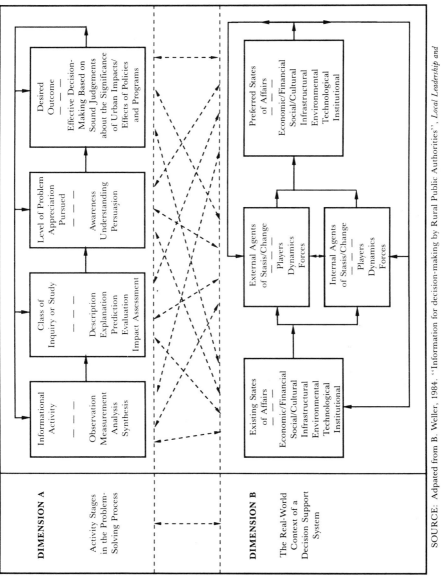

DIMENSION A

Activity Stages in the Problem-Solving Process

DIMENSION B

The Real-World Context of a Decision Support System

SOURCE: Adpated from B. Weller, 1984. "Information for decision-making by Rural Public Authorities", *Local Leadership and Rural Development*, Washington: USDA, Extension Service and Economic Research Service, p. 37.

The significance of consequences (impacts/effects) would ideally be spelled out in an "ex ante" manner as part of the Preferred States of Affairs using a normative approach. Lack of full definition in that regard does not preclude making judgements in an "ex post" manner, however, about what should be or should have been. Indeed, given the widespread reality of decision-making with imperfect information even about what is, it would be extraordinary to impose "full normatism" as a condition of the model's validity and utility.

On the other hand, judgements can be made about the significance of urban impacts/effects associated with a continuation or extension of Existing States of Affairs. There are, of course, shortcomings to the incrementalist approach, as documented elsewhere.[6] The fact remains, however, that in the real world context (Dimension B) of decision support systems, many decisions are made without a Preferred State of Affairs prospective in which to cast judgements.

For the purposes of the present paper, distinctions are made between the normative or incrementalist setting of policy and policy research initiatives under a special circumstance: that is, when the distinction is explicitly built into the initiative(s) by the responsible officers or units. Credit of that sort is due, if only to acknowledge that the distinction was appreciated by those responsible for the initiative(s).

UIA IN A POLICY FORMATION CONTEXT

Figure 2 serves to illustrate at a general level the variety of circumstances and situations which confronted and perplexed the Ministry.

All of the words and terms referred to as "Components" or "Elements" in Figure 2 can be found somewhere in the Ministry's literature, or were part of the MSUA vocabulary. To my knowledge, however, and on the basis of a review of hundreds of policy formation and policy research documents, there are no previous models or frameworks which a) spelled out the Components/Elements, or b) presented the Components/Elements within a policy formation model or framework, a la Figure 2.

As an *indication*, therefore, of the UIA presence at the Ministry, as recorded in its documentation—Minister's speeches, speeches of officials, work programs, research reports, consultants' reports, annual or year-end reports, Cabinet Documents, Etc.—only two Components

FIGURE 2. COMPONENTS AND ELEMENTS TO CONSIDER IN EXAMINING THE PROCESS, CONTENT, AND DIRECTION OF URBAN POLICY FORMATION IN A FEDERAL SYSTEM

COMPONENTS	ELEMENTS
Government Players in the Urban Policy Process	Federal/Central State/Provincial Regional/Local
Status of Government Authority for Urban Policy	Centralized Centralizing Joint Devolving Devolved
Urban Policy Approach/Philosophy	Dirigisme Accommodation Laissez-Faire
Urban Policy Reference	Explicit Implicit
Urban Policy Impacts	Direct Indirect
Urban Policy Objectives	Efficiency Equity Quality of Life . . .
Urban Policy Domain-Spatial	Urbanization Urban Systems Urban Places . . .
Urban Policy Domain-Sectoral	Economic Social Cultural Environmental . . .
Urban Policy Instruments	Programs Plans Regulations Controls By-Laws . . .
Urban Policy Variables	Interest Rates/Taxes/Loans/Grants/Immigration Levels/ Land Use Density/Zoning/Pollution Indexes/Social Service Levels/. . ./. . ./. . .

*Source: Adpated from B. Wellar, 1984. ''National Urban Policy in the Coming Decades: Structural and Functional Adjustment to Settlement Systems by Dirigisme, Accommodation or Laissez-Faire? Second World Regional Science Conference, Netherlands Economic Institute, Erasmus University, Rotterdam, The Netherlands, June 4-15, 1984. Ottawa: Department of Geography, University of Ottawa.

are used to review and examine the status of the UIA perspective at the Ministry: Urban Policy Domain-Spatial, and Urban Policy Domain-Sectoral.[7]

Within the Spatial Component, the following Elements are considered: urbanization, urban systems; and urban places. The first term, urbanization is explicitly referenced in the Proclamation,[8] whereas the latter two are broadly interpreted to represent what was meant/intended by the Government of Canada (in a spatial sense) in its policy charge to the agency.[9]

As for the Sectoral Component, the Elements selected are "arbitrary" in that the Proclamation provided no direction whatsoever in this regard, other than a vague reference to "urban environment". Some may argue that the reference to "urban environment" is not vague but, if so, then what is one to make of a 1974 interpretation that the term "was intended to refer to urban affairs generally, i.e., to the whole spectrum of activities of the Ministry"?[10]

The task, then, is to review and examine the UIA presence at MSUA in terms of the selected policy formation Components and Elements, and associated policy research efforts. Of interest is the degree and extent that policy and policy research at MSUA were concerned with assessing or judging the significance—in economic, social or environmental terms—of consequences arising from policy and policy research initiatives related to urbanization, urban systems, and urban places.

THE UIA PRESENCE AT MSUA, 1971-1979: A SAMPLER

The term "sampler" is chosen advisedly. That is, access to hundreds of documents notwithstanding, it is inevitable that documents were overlooked, even for the years 1972-1979 when I was with the Ministry in the Research (Policy Research, etc. Branch or) Wing.[11]

A combined narrative and tabular format is used to structure the review and examination of the UIA presence at the Ministry. A distinction is made between the UIA presence "In Principle" and "In Practice", and the documentation examined is grouped as follows:

1. Minister's Office;
2. Office of Secretary;
3. Office of Assistant Secretary of Policy, Research, Policy Research or Policy and Research Wing;

4. Policy, Research, Policy Research, or Policy and Research Branch; and
5. A separate section on the Senior Inter-Departmental Committee on Urban Affairs (SIDCUA) which cut across all of the groupings in 1) to 4) above.

The text which follows briefly reports on the general nature of the UIA presence for each grouping. Particular comments are reserved for documents reporting on events, activities etc. which notably affected the status of or respect for the UIA presence within one of the groups, or across the agency. Footnotes are used for including these comments.

Minister's Office

It is appropriate to begin this section by establishing whether it is *reasonable* to expect a UIA presence within the Minister's Office. That is, it would be unfair to examine documents for a UIA presence in an "ex poste" manner if it was not reasonable to expect such a presence in the first place.

Three documents are deemed sufficient to make the case.[12] First, on a politician-to-politician basis, the *Report of the Task Force on Housing and Urban Development*, under the direction of Paul Hellyer (1969), then Minister of Transport, made a number of explicit and implicit references to the *significance of consequences* arising from both the do-nothing and do-something scenarios of federal "participation" related to urbanization, urban systems, and urban places.

Second, and also on a politician-to-politician basis, Robert Andras, then Minister of Housing, picked up on a number of the Task Force themes in an Address to the Canadian Institute of Public Affairs in early 1970. The Andras address contains a number of explicit and implicit references to the significance of urban consequences flowing from both policy action and inaction.[13]

And, third, the Economic Council (1967) in its *Fourth Annual Review* provided a considerable amount of "advice" to the federal government on the policy implications of rapid urban growth in particular, and urban problems and prospects in particular. Again, frequent explicit and implicit references were made to the significance of urban consequences associated with policy impacts and effects.

As shown in Table 1, UIA became established in rather dramatic fashion at the Ministerial level in 1974 when Barney Danson became Minister.

Review of Danson's speeches, for example, reveals frequent references to the economic, social and/or environmental significance associated with the issues or concerns of the day—urban concentration, growth (amount and rate) of urban centres—and the resulting impact/effects of scarcity of agricultural land, small town and rural area de-population, high housing costs, overcrowding, pollution, etc.

That Danson would have had an interest in or proclivity for the UIA perspective is not surprising. He pursued that theme in his Notes for a Panel on urban Problems, "Our Urban Concern—One Federal Viewpoint", prepared for a public meeting in his York North constituency in 1970. In other words, Danson was in a "UIA mode" well before he became Minister of State for Urban Affairs.

Further, and as evidenced by material produced prior to, during and after the Habitat Conference in Vancouver in 1976 (which is a long way from a public meeting in York North), he kept the UIA faith.[14]

During the other regimes (those of Robert Andras and Ron Basford prior to Danson, and Andre Ouellet after), the significance of urban consequences were in large part measured in very narrow political terms, rather than in their broader economic, social and/or environmental contexts. That is, at the outset of the agency, and his 1970 remarks now history, Andras' inputs and outputs were primarily oriented towards establishing the rationale of the Ministry. Basford, in turn, wanted the Ministry to be seen to be doing things and thereby gathering political points (for himself and the government).[15]

Ouellet, as seen at the time and even more so in retrospect, seemed to perceive the Ministry in a program sense: that is, as an agency capable of helping the government create "jobs, jobs, jobs", and perform other such works.[16] In that regard, even the relatively few documents with a UIA reference that were encountered probably over-state Ouellet's interest in the economic, social or environmental significance of urban consequences arising from the Ministry's policy/policy research effort. That is, the UIA presence as a "guiding light" was more likely an ill-appreciated legacy bequeathed by Danson than any creation or internalized concept held by Ouellet.

Only during Danson's period as Minister, then, was the Minister's Office tuned in to ascertaining and judging the significance of consequences associated with the Ministry's policy/policy research effort. Indeed, by his example, Danson gave policy/policy research "advice" to his officials on the importance of dealing at the significance-of-consequences level.

TABLE 1. NUMBER OF REFERENCES TO URBAN IMPACT
ASSESSMENT[1]: DOCUMENTS OF MINISTER'S OFFICE, 1971-1979

	YEAR								
	'71	'72	'73	'74	'75	'76	'77	'78	'79
Number of Documents Reviewed[2]	4	8	8	12	20	26	30	21	5
Number of Documents with UIA Reference	1	2	1	7	9	8	9	5	1
In Principle[3]	1	2	1	6	7	6	6	4	1
In Practice[4]	0	0	0	1	2	2	3	1	0

NOTES

1. A UIA reference in this paper means that consideration was given to the significance (economic, social, environmental) or urban consequences (impacts and effects) associated with or arising from the policy/research/ policy research effort of the Ministry.
2. Documents include speechs, monographs, annual reports, etc., issued under the Minister's authority, and for which the presence of UIA reference was a *reasonable* expectation.
3. References to UIA "In Principle" refers to statements that the UIA perspective (with its significance of consequence(s) condition) should, must, will be respected, considered etc. in the policy/research/policy research effort of the Ministry.
4. References to UIA "In Practice" refers to the (actual) application of the UIA perspective (with its significance of consequence(s) condition) in the policy/research/policy research effort of the Ministry. In those cases where UIA was referenced both "In Principle" and "In Practice", the document was asigned to the "In Practice" row.

Secretary's Office

There are obvious political and administrative ties between the Minister and Secretary which call for much of their deliberations to be more off than on the record. Hence, it is difficult, to say the least, to determine from afar (in distance and time) the views which they held about the Ministry's mandate or mission, and why and how the agency might best proceed. As a result, this review and examination of documents from the Secretary's Office is heavily qualified. That is, what is observable and countable by no means reflects all that a Secretary might have had to endure, or might have wished to have happen, in trying to achieve a productive convergence between a Minister's needs on the one hand, and the Ministry's policy/policy research capabilities on the other.[17] Having acknowledged the "Secretary's Bind", let us review and examine the UIA presence in the Office of the Secretary.

As suggested by Table 2, and likely due to the influence of Danson as Minister, the "maturing" of the agency's grasp of the policy process, and the surge of effort induced by Habitat, a strong UIA presence was in place in the 1974-1976 period.[18] It is also noteworthy that the Secretary during this period, J.W. MacNeill, came to the Ministry with a strong background in environmental matters, and he brought a significance of consequences sense to the position.

During the formative years, the Secretary was Peter Oberlander, who brought an academic, planning-oriented background to the position. It was Oberlander's circumstance to be caught between the external "hard-ball" politics of the day—other federal agencies did not

TABLE 2. NUMBER OF REFERENCES TO URBAN IMPACT ASSESSMENT[1]: DOCUMENTS OF SECRETARY'S OFFICE, 1971-1979

	YEAR								
	'71	'72	'73	'74	'75	'76	'77	'78	'79
Number of Documents Reviewed[2]	6	9	13	17	31[5]	31[5]	8	8	4
Number of Documents with UIA Reference	3	3	5	8	15	16	2	1	1
In Principle[3]	3	3	5	6	12	13	2	1	1
In Practice[4]	0	0	0	2	3	3	0	0	0

NOTES

1. As in Table 1.
2. Documents include speeches, monographs, annual reports, policy/research/ policy research work program statements, Treasury Board submissions, etc. issued under the Secretary's authority, and for which the presence of a UIA reference was a *reasonable* expectation.
3. As in Table 1.
4. As in Table 1.
5. The *Urban Prospects Papers,* prepared for the Habitat Conference in Vancouver in 1976, are included in these columns of figures.

take kindly to being coordinated,[19] and certainly not by a newcomer-on-the-block, junior agency—and the internal "hard-ball" politics of the day—reconciling diverse and strongly-held views about the substance and direction of the Ministry's policy and policy research effort. It is to Oberlander's credit that the Secretary's Office managed to offer at least a flavour of UIA in its outputs.

In comparison to the MacNeill years, those of William Teron (1975-1979) were far less productive in terms of documentation, and were far less attentive to the UIA perspective.[20]

The years 1977-1979 reflected in part a loss of UIA momentum, indeed any momentum that drew on intellectual capital, due to the seemingly interminable re-organizations and shuffles visited upon the agency in 1975-76, and on-and-off throughout 1977 and 1978. The demise of a UIA presence within the Secretary's Office was also likely due in part to Teron's disdain for what he perceived to be "academic research", and his preference (as stated in 1976) for such non-UIA activities as developing standards and criteria of urban quality (shades of turning the research clock back 3 or 4 years), and acting as federal broker for urban matters with the provinces and their municipalities (shades of turning the Tri-Level Conference clock back 2 or 3 years).[21]

In summary, UIA as a guiding light within the Secretary's Office flickered, shone brightly, and went out, all in a space of about eight years.

Office of Assistant Secretary

The policy/policy research agenda for much of the Ministry's life was set by Harvey Lithwick prior to and during his tenure as the Ministry's first Assistant Secretary.[22] Examination of documents produced by or for Lithwick reveal an immediate concern with the consequences of interventions (or lack thereof), and in particular with their economic significance. Further, in the documents considered, and those produced after his departure, Lithwick demonstrated a keen sense—if not explicitly phrased as such—for a UIA perspective as the so-called bottom line for research in a policy context, and for policy in the context of urbanization/urban systems/urban places (1982). In Lithwick's work, then, UIA was a theme, and not just a casual reference.

MacNeill, who succeeded Lithwick as Assistant Secretary, brought an environmental as opposed to economic orientation to the Wing, and a sense for the UIA perspective. The Assistant Secretary's Office under

Paul Tellier and Hubert Laframboise, and due more likely to Mac-Neill's influence as Secretary than their own proclivities, maintained at least a low-level UIA presence in the years 1973-1975.[23]

As for the years 1975-76-77, when the agency's flip-overs[24] matched those of a pancake house, UIA (which requires a strong sense of commitment, perspective, and direction to prevail), began its demise within the Assistant Secretary's Office. By 1978, after several years with Lorenz Schmidt at the helm, numerous re-inventions of various and sundry policy research and policy research wheels, and the loss of many talented urban thinkers and researchers, the UIA presence was a shadow of its former self. (See Table 3.)

In summary, UIA, in the Assistant Secretary's Office went from the status of "modus vivendi"—the guiding light—at the outset of the Ministry, to a position of non-status—the light had gone out—when the Ministry was itself extinguished in 1979.

Policy and Research Branch

If space and time had permitted, the policy formation and policy research efforts would have been separated for the following reasons.

First, it does not necessarily follow that completed, methodologically-based research is a pre-condition for postulating or declaring the significance of consequences arising from policy or program initiatives, or lack thereof.

Second, not all research effort was translated, or was intended to be translated into policy research or policy.

Third, research outputs tended to be policy inputs when convergences fortuitously occurred, rather than being simultaneously-arrived-at, intended outcomes.[25] Hence, to reveal the nature of research and policy relationships, when and where they existed, the chain-of-events (a la evaluation) would preferably be tracked rather than presumed.

Fourth, there were distinct differences and challenges, respectively, in the research and policy capabilities of Ministry staff,[26] and the environments and constituencies associated with the respective domains.

Finally, a number of Ministry personnel were involved in both research and policy activities, administratively, and in terms of substance. Hence, a third grouping of policy research would be required to adequately distinguish among policy-research arrangements vis-a-vis respect for and attention to the UIA perspective.

What follows is the status of UIA at the policy and research level in the Ministry. (Table 4). In large measure, the pattern within the Branch was similar to those noted above for the other groupings, but with two notable differences.

First, the proportion of documents with a UIA reference range from higher to considerably higher. Second, and notwithstanding the seemingly endless turmoil and institutional change elsewhere in the agency, the UIA perspective was a continuing presence in the Branch throughout the life of the agency, and even in 1977 and 1978 when deepthinking was decidedly not the order of the day within the Ministry's Executive.

Since it is not possible to review and examine all years in detail, one program year (1974-75) has been selected to illustrate the kind of production environment in which the Branch operated. Further, one program year (1973-74) has been selected to illustrate the nature of the UIA presence at the Ministry.

The basis of the latter illustration is contained in the documentation prepared for the "Montebello Retreat", at which a number of Theme Statements were prepared and discussed by Research Staff. The "Retreat" was organized by Len Gertler, then Director-General, Research Branch.

A total of 18 theme statements, in varying stages of development were considered: 1) Land Markets, 2) Housing Markets, 3) Urban Growth, 4) Demography, 5) MUPIM (Macro-urban Program Impact Model), 6) Man and Built Environment, 7) Urban Crowding, 8) Environmental Health, 9) Inner City, 10) Technology-Environment, 11) Urban Government Systems, 12) Citizen Participation, 13) Urban Public Economy, 14) Environmental Quality, 15) Urban Open Space, 16) Values and Structures, 17) Urban Systems, and 18) Urban Information (MSUA, 1973b).

Each of the eighteen themes contained an explicit reference to observing, measuring, analysing or synthesizing the impacts and effects of urban consequences arising from interventions or lack thereof; in addition, in the majority of statements explicit reference was made to the significance of those consequences.[27]

Further, it was my experience, and it has been borne out by the documentation review, that many of the researchers at MSUA appreciated the desirability of building a UIA perspective into their research or policy research efforts.[28]

As for the reference to the production environment, the work

TABLE 3. NUMBER OF REFERENCES TO URBAN IMPACT ASSESSMENT[1]: DOCUMENTS OF OFFICE OF ASSISTANT SECRETARY FOR POLICY, POLICY RESEARCH OR POLICY AND RESEARCH WING[2], 1971-1979

	YEAR								
	'71	'72	'73	'74	'75	'76	'77	'78	'79
Number of Documents Reviewed[3]	8	12	19	31	36	41	30	16	8
Number of Documents with UIA Reference	5	5	6	10	11	12	7	4	2
In Principle[4]	5	5	4	5	6	9	5	3	2
In Practice[5]	0	0	2	5	5	4	2	1	0

NOTES

1. As in Table 1.
2. The Ministry appeared to be re-organized with each change in Minister, or Secretary, and more than once within some administrations; hence the various appellations.
3. Documents include speeches, monographs, annual reports, policy/research/ policy research work program statements, (Draft) Treasury Board Submissions, etc., issued under the Assistant Secretary's authority, and for which the presence of a UIA reference was a *reasonable* expectation.
4. Same as note 3 in Table 1.
5. Same as note 4 in Table 1.

TABLE 4. NUMBER OF REFERENCES TO URBAN IMPACT ASSESSMENT[1]: DOCUMENTS OF POLICY, POLICY RESEARCH OR POLICY AND RESEARCH BRANCH[2], 1971-1979

	YEAR								
	'71	'72	'73	'74	'75	'76	'77	'78	'79
Number of Documents Reviewed[3]	13	27	56	69	85	94	70	49	21
Number of Documents with UIA Reference	4	6	17	26	32	26	23	17	8
In Principle[4]	4	6	13	10	20	24	17	14	6
In Practice[5]	0	0	4	10	12	12	6	3	2

NOTES
1. As in Table 1.
2. As in Table 3.
3. Documents include (draft) speeches, monographs, policy/research/policy research work statements, policy papers, policy and research papers position papers, (Draft) Cabinet Documents, research papers/reports, etc., produced by Branch directorates or groups, and for which the presence of a UIA reference was a *reasonable* expectation.
4. Same as note 3 in Table 1.
5. Same as note 4 in Table 1.

program for 1974-75 dispels any vague, pejorative notions about "ivory towerism" or research for the sake of research within the Policy and Research Branch.[29] The Work Program contains among other products, 22 Research Reports, 3 Reports on Impact Guidelines, 13 Policy Papers, 16 Research and Policy papers, 1 Green Paper, and *eleven* (11) Cabinet Documents.

It is probably fair to say that no documents intended for Cabinet left the Research or Policy and Research Branch without a UIA reference during the period of 1973-1976, and that a similar commitment held within the Directorates of the Policy Analysis Wing after 1976, problems at the "receiving end" within the Ministry notwithstanding.[30]

As a summary comment, UIA was an abiding concern within the Policy and Research Branch throughout the life of the agency, and particularly during the "deep-think" period of 1972-1976.

Senior Inter-Departmental Committee on Urban Affairs (SIDCUA)

Review of the SIDCUA documentation which I was able to obtain (memoranda, calls for ideas, SIDCUA minutes, draft reports, agency comments) for 1974, 1975, 1976 and 1977 reveals that the "bottom-up" contributions (from the Policy and Research Branch or Directorate levels) usually contained a UIA reference as to the significance (economic, social, environmental) of urban consequences arising from federal department activities. Materials of a "top-down" nature, on the other hand, and especially the internal documents, worried a great deal about such matters as which agencies should sit at the SIDCUA table, the shape of the table, who should chair meetings, the review process, etc.

Small wonder, therefore, that the Ministry had difficulty getting a handle on, much less organizing Canada's affairs urban—urbanization, urban systems, urban places—it couldn't even get a handle on much less organize the inter-departmental committee critical to the Ministry's mandate and life!

There is one other aspect of SIDCUA that is useful as a means to distinguish between the executive and policy research levels, vis-a-vis their respect for and attention to UIA. It warrants being noted as a capsule comment for other SIDCUA-type endeavours.

Contrary to what the "ivory tower" label might have connoted for the Ministry's research staff, and particularly for those with advanced degrees or university teaching experience, the evidence is that they understood, and their work largely respected, the importance of being relevant. The evidence in this regard is the general tendency in the research and policy research documentation to deal with the significance of consequences, and to focus on the economic, social and environmental aspects of those consequences.

At the executive level, however, and especially during the years of the Teron regime (1975-79), SIDCUA appears to be, and was perceived by outsiders to be, an instrument of empire building. The evidence in this regard includes: 1) the "turf holding" approach of executives in other departments, notwithstanding that appreciation of and respect for urban implications could have strengthened their departments' contributions to the federal (and national) system; and 2) the largely bureaucratic as opposed to subject matter or substantive orientation of SIDCUA materials produced by some of the Ministry's Executive groups. In other words, UIA became expendable in the face of real and perceived departmental posturing and opportunism, including that of the Ministry.

Perhaps, as some have claimed, there were "ivory towers" at MSUA, but if so, they had quite different impacts. That is, the academic one gave the Ministry its ideas, and its life, whereas the bureaucratic one eschewed ideas, and caused the agency to atrophy. SIDCUA, then, was a compound failure: when the bureaucratic tower fell it took the academic tower with it.

In terms of what the open literature says on the subject of the UIA presence in urban departments or agencies in other countries,[31] UIA at MSUA would have scored 7 or possibly 8 on a scale of ten during the years 1971-1975. Had that tendency continued, by 1979 the Ministry of State for Urban Affairs might well have been an internationally recognized guiding light in the field of urban impact assessment.

Instead, both UIA and MSUA flickered and burned brightly, and dimmed, and flickered, and . . .

COMMENTS ON THE MINISTRY'S DSS PROGRESS

This section briefly considers the Ministry's informational inquiry and problem appreciation progress over the nine years. The purpose of the DSS reference is two-fold:

1) The DSS context provided by Figure 1 is instructive as a mechanism for relating the strength of the Ministry's knowledge base to its UIA judgements. In brief, judgements off the top of one's head (intuition, common sense) are not likely to carry the same substantive weight as those derived via robust and rigorous informational activities, and inquiries. The Ministry's progress towards the latter basis of decision-making is elaborated.

2) The DSS context of Figure 1 illustrates that informational activities and inquiries are inputs to the larger UIA problematique of the Ministry: that is, to expand awareness, further understanding, and/or influence decisions. The Ministry's record vis-a-vis problem appreciation is reviewed in terms of the attention given to the three stages, and hence its DSS progress as a policy change agent.

Progress in Informational Activities and Levels of Inquiry[32]

The Policy and Research Branch (or variations thereof) was to provide the substantive base of the Ministry's overall effort, in both its external and internal respects. Since the progress of the Branch may be considered as a surrogate for the Ministry's progress (regarding Informational Activities and Levels of Inquiry) it is used as an indicator of the Ministry's progress towards achieving a substantive knowledge base.

As shown in Table 5, the policy/policy research effort in the Branch has been allocated among Observation, Measurement, Analysis and Synthesis. The allocations are based on a combination of:

1) The proportion of documents concerned explicitly with each sub-activity; and

2) The relative emphasis given to the sub-activities in documents which dealt with more than one of them.

The final column in Table 5 is proposed as an approximation of where the Ministry should have been by 1979 if:

1) Its policy/policy research performance had lived up to its original promise; and

2) The Ministry "experiment" had been structured along the lines of experimental design.

While there may be differences of opinion about the final column of Table 5, it is anticipated that they would not markedly alter the assessments in a general sense.

TABLE 5. ALLOCATION (IN PER CENT) OF EFFORT BY THE POLICY AND RESEARCH BRANCH TO INFORMATIONAL ACTIVITIES, 1971-1979

INFORMATIONAL ACTIVITY	YEAR									Expected Status After 9 Years
	'71	'72	'73	'74	'75	'76	'77	'78	'79	
Observation	40	35	30	30	30	60	55	55	55	20
Measurement	25	30	35	35	30	25	25	25	25	30
Analysis	25	25	25	25	30	10	15	15	15	30
Synthesis	10	10	10	10	15	5	5	5	5	20

On the basis of the documents reviewed, by 1975 the Branch had achieved a "reasonable" Informational Activity profile. The Observational aspect was being reduced, a Measurement flourish had occurred in 1972-73, Analysis was solidly confirmed, and Synthesis, which by its nature yeilds no more than grudging progress at the best of times, had gained a measure of presence.

In late 1975, and in 1976, the policy/policy research effort returned to the "square one" phase of Informational Activity. The research tradition that had been built up over the preceding five years largely evaporated, few established researchers remained, and quality research— much of which had satisfied the conditions of methodological design— fell off dramatically. In brief, between 1975 and 1979 the Informational Activity part of the Branch (re-titled Policy Analysis with a series of Directorates) far more reflected a re-invention of a low-level policy/ policy research wheel than any acceleration or momentum of the policy/policy research vehicle taken over in 1975.

By 1979, the situation had changed only marginally: that is, despite a four-year opportunity, the policy/policy research effort was still in low gear, even to the point of not using previous work that was on the shelf for the taking.

In summary, for a few years the Ministry's progress in Informational Activity matched its original promise, only to fall into disarray in its later years.

As for progress related to Level of Inquiry, the general position was similar. The "Easy" Description work was reduced over the 1971-1975 period, the central policy/policy research activities of Explanation and Prediction were established from the outset of the agency, and maintained, and the more demanding task of Evaluation was accorded a reasonable amount of attention. (Table 6)

TABLE 6. ALLOCATION (IN PER CENT) OF EFFORT BY THE POLICY AND RESEARCH BRANCH TO INQUIRY ACTIVITIES BY LEVEL EXCLUDING IMPACT ASSESSMENT, 1971-1979

LEVEL OF INQUIRY	YEAR									Expected Status After 9 Years
	'71	'72	'73	'74	'75	'76	'77	'78	'79	
Description	60	55	50	50	45	75	65	60	60	20
Explanation	15	20	20	17.5	20	12.5	12.5	12.5	12.5	30
Prediction	20	20	20	17.5	20	12.5	12.5	12.5	12.5	30
Evaluation	5	5	10	15	15	5	5	5	10	20

In late 1975 and throughout 1976, however, and as noted above, the policy/policy research wheel was re-invented, and a return to Description took hold. That Explanation and Prediction did not get reduced to even lower levels than those shown was likely due to two factors:

1) Some researchers had managed to cultivate a "demand" for such work among clients external to the Ministry, which made further cuts risky for the Executive; and,

2) Officers with an inquiry "bent" managed to build explanation and prediction aspects into what might have appeared to be descriptive work.[33]

With respect to the Evaluation aspect, which seeks to establish the consequences (impacts and effects) of interventions, its fate was largely defined by SIDCUA's performance. That is, SIDCUA set the upper limit on what was achieved in practice by Evaluation studies. SIDCUA, after a period of less-than-robust health prior to 1975, atrophied in the Offices of the Secretary/Assistant Secretary (Policy Analysis) in the post 1975-76 period, and Evaluation succumbed due to lack of interest and action.

In summary, up until 1975 the Ministry exhibited reasonable progress towards achieving a substantive body of knowledge upon which to base UIA judgements. The Ministry could legitimately claim, I suggest, to have established itself on substantive grounds as *the* federal government's urban voice, if not yet an authority on affairs urban. By the time of the close of the Ministry, however, the quality of the policy/policy research effort, when measured in terms of methodological criteria, was at best only marginally better than that which prevailed back in 1971.

Progress in Problem Appreciation

The logical progression of this aspect of a DSS approach is, in brief: 1) make them aware; 2) make them understand; and, 3) persuade them to see things our way.

Given the Ministry's lack of programs, and hence lack of money—one of the ultimate persuaders in life—the agency's Problem Appreciation weapons were two-fold:

First, political clout; second, sweet reason, represented by facts, argumentation, and the authority vested in its experts.

If an agency lacks political clout, and in large part that was the Ministry's situation, then "sweet reason" forms the heart of the agency's awareness, understanding and, ultimately, persuasive capability. This part of the paper briefly reviews and examines the Executive function's performance (as a surrogate for the Ministry) in the Problem Appreciation phase.

As illustrated by Table 7, the literature search uncovered some disconcerting aspects of this phase, and particularly in view of the Ministry's lack of political (and upper-level bureaucratic) clout.

TABLE 7. ALLOCATION (IN PER CENT) OF EFFORT BY THE EXECUTIVE (MINISTER, SECRETARY, ASSISTANT SECRETARY) TO LEVELS OF PROBLEM APPRECIATION, 1971-1979

LEVEL OF PROBLEM APPRECIATION	YEAR									Expected Status After 9 Years
	'71	'72	'73	'74	'75	'76	'77	'78	'79	
Awareness	60	60	55	45	40	70	65	65	65	15
Understanding	20	30	35	40	40	15	15	15	15	55
Persuasion	20	10	15	15	20	15	20	20	20	30

Third, and perhaps this was due to frequent changes to the Executive, and/or lack of urban expertise among its members, but the emphasis on Awareness throughout the duration suggests that that was the level of problem appreciation characteristic of the Executive groups themselves. That is, the learning curve of the Executive was by no means monotonically increasing; instead, the learning curve dropped each time a regime or key executive required becoming acquainted with the subject matter and politics (external/internal) of the Ministry, with two unfortunate outcomes: Awareness exercises (briefings) became the order of the day/week/month, or Persuasion was attempted without having mastered the preceding Awareness and Understanding phases.

And, fourth, in terms of modelling how the Executive should have evolved in a Problem Appreciation mode, the 1972-1975 period suggests an ''era'' during which the Executive had a handle on what was necessary in order to win friends and influence people using sweet reason:

1) There was an abiding, high degree of attention to Understanding as the key to the Ministry's knowledge base, and its influence base;

2) Less emphasis was placed on Awareness as Understanding took root among the Ministry's constituents; And,

3) There was a modest increase in attempts at Persuasion.

This latter development reflected, perhaps, the lag between the phases—it takes time for policy formation/policy research outcomes to move from being accepted as ''right'' in principle to being accepted as the right thing to do in practice—and an increased appreciation of the Ministry's need to be more selective and prepared in its attempts at effecting change.

To summarize this section on the Ministry's progress in a DSS context, respect for such a context (when it occurred) happened as much or more by accident or chance than by design. Major prices to be paid as a result of the numerous disruptions and re-directions of the organization were two-fold: 1) a lack of flow in the policy formation/ policy research effort; and 2) a seemingly eternal mis-match between the quality of the policy research knowledge base and the quality of purpose to which that base was put by the Executive.

Small wonder, therefore, that the Ministry had difficulty giving direction to Canada's urban affairs: it had great difficulty charting and following its own policy formation/policy research path.

CONCLUSION

This paper reviewed and examined the urban impact assessment (UIA) presence at the Ministry of State for Urban Affairs. The materials used to determine the status and nature of the UIA presence were Ministry documents—speeches, annual reports, work programs, monographs, policy papers, research studies, (Draft) Cabinet Documents, memoranda, Letters of Agreement, conference papers, journal and proceedings papers, etc. The following general themes appear to be supportable by the literature search and content analysis.

First, the urban impact assessment perspective was by no means a guiding light that burned brilliantly and continuously throughout the Ministry, at a point in time or over time.

Rather, the UIA concept manifested its presence in two less pervasive, less beacon-like ways. In a top-down sense, reference to the significance of consequences provided the Minister and the Executive with the necessary language to occasionally exhort external players (and Ministry staff) to think about and weigh the ultimate outcomes of interventions, or lack thereof.

In a bottom-up sense, on the other hand, the UIA concept provided a dimension of relevance not afforded by other levels of inquiry. That is, when time and circumstances permitted, attempting to bring to bear all required resources and expertise in order to judge the significance of an intervention—in real-world terms—provided an ultimate policy formation/policy research challenge.

That UIA was neither the modus vivendi nor modus operandi of the Ministry should not, in practical terms, be surprising. The field of impact assessment (IA) was itself only several decades old, and it was not until the 1960s that IA began to take on its urban aspects.

Hence, it was not unreasonable that UIA as a branch of IA was not incorporated on a first principles basis throughout the agency. Indeed, given the magnitude of the task set for the Ministry, which literally was created and set down in the midst of "the urban problem", some praise is due for the extent of UIA presence that was achieved under the "rush-rush" circumstances.

Further, in the vein of reality, the derivation of research—based consequences frequently took more time than the political system liked to allow, or accepted. Remembering to assess or judge the significance (economic, social, environmental) of consequences in the face of such pressure prompts the recollection of an apt and off-muttered phrase: "When you are up to your ass in alligators it's hard to remember that you were told to drain the swamp". There were a lot of "alligators" for the policy/policy research group to deal with prior to assessing or judging the significance of consequences, as too frequently the urgent prevailed over the important.

Second, by 1974/75 the Ministry's decision support system mentality and capability had matured considerably. It is quite possible that in the subsequent years, had the UIA progress continued, the Ministry would have acquired a formidable UIA capacity. That it did not evolve in such a preferred manner had little or nothing to do with UIA per se, and virtually everything to do with those who chose to put their personal stamps or slants on the Ministry.

I close by noting that Canada's "urban affair" is far from over, and particularly in view of the fact that many of our urban places are in a re-planning stage. Further, the forces of urbanization and urban systems are far from spent. As a result, there will continue to be a flow of economic, social and environmental consequences as a result of interventions, or their lack, and for which we as a nation are ill-equipped to assess or judge in terms of their significance.

Perhaps this paper will have served a valuable secondary purpose if it succeeds in persuading others to report on their sense of the UIA experience at the Ministry. That kind of documentation might prove to be a most important contribution for the Ministry to make as an outcome of an urban policy formation/policy research experiment. After all, given history's insistence on repeating itself, would it not be wise to begin preparing now for the next version of the MSUA experiment?

NOTES

1. In a previous related paper by Wellar (1982), an urban impact assessment perspective was used to examine public policy processes in Canada for the period 1968-1982. The "targets" in that paper were three levels of government (federal, provincial, municipal). The task was to establish, in general terms, the purposes, ways and extent that urban impact assessment was incorporated, in principle and in practice, in the policy processes of those levels of government. Wellar, Barry. 1982. "Urban Impact Assessment in Public Policy Processes: The Canadian Record, 1968-1972" in Len Gertler

(ed.). *The Canadian Journal of Regional Science*. (Special Issue on Public Policy—
Urban and Regional Issues), 39-65.

2. Among the many media pieces on this topic are several recent newspaper
articles which illustrate the institutional and substantive range of impact
assessment activities and concerns. One article, "Economic Council too slow,
irrelevant, ineffective, MPs Complain", *The Gazette* (Montreal, June 18, 1986)
questions the Council's impact on public policy, and could have been written
about MSUA. The Council should heed what happened to the Ministry. On
the other hand, two articles reporting on the United Nations International
Conference on Population and the Urban Future, held in Barcelona, Spain,
May 19-22, 1986 touched almost every urban impact assessment base. Upon
reading "The demoralizing dimensions of urban growth" and "Megacity
maladies cry out for a cure" *Toronto Star*, May 18, 1986 and May 25, 1986,
respectively), many former MSUA officials might believe that they are in a
time warp: most if not all the concerns, issues, problems, recommendations
were raised at the Ministry, or at Habitat a decade ago!

3. Ibid.

4. As noted later in the text, Canada's "urban problem" and that of many
other countries seemingly moves further away from even partial resolution
with each passing day. MSUA was an "experiment" in large measure, and as
such there is a researcher's obligation to report on findings, and especially
those involving the significance of consequences, of things going wrong, or
being set right.

5. See the excellent paper by Steger and Lakshmanan in Hemmens, George
(ed.) *Urban Development Models*, (Special Report 97), Highway Research Board,
Washington, 1968, and especially the numerous references to UIA. See also
Wellar (1981, 1982).

6. The long-running, normative-incrementalist argument is admirably
summarized by Cooke, Philip. *Theories of Planning and Spatial Development*.
London: Hutchinson. 1983. For materials produced by the Ministry on this
topic see, for example, the following: Cameron et al. 91972), MSUA (1972),
MSUA (1973a, 1973c), Seni (1973), Swain (1972) and Wellar and Levallee
(1976) in *Appendix A* at the end of the book.

7. Other Components/Elements are discussed in Wellar (1982, 1986) and in
many of the MSUA documents referenced in the text and in Appendix A.

8. For the substantive portion of the Proclamation see *The Canada Gazette*,
July 10, 1971.

9. Readers may find the following, brief aside on the Government of
Canada's spatial sense amusing. As noted in the 1982 UIA paper (Wellar,
1982, 51-52), a number of agencies claimed to have little or no urban impact
associated with their policies and programs, and received a similar series of
responses. Which begs the question: if federal policies and programs have

neither urban nor rural impacts, then exactly *where* in Canada do federal policies and programs have impacts and create effects?

10. MSUA (1974b, p. 17). Since reference to the significance of consequences arising from "the whole spectrum of activities of the Ministry" is beyond my comprehension, the UIA perspective is limited to the following Elements: First, the economic and the social, which are matters of abiding concern to all governments at all times, and are invariably referenced in association with such policy objectives as efficiency and equity; and Second, the environmental, in respect of its being mentioned in the Proclamation. The term is less grandly defined here, though, and pertains just to the built environment and its implications, for example, for the Quality of Life Element in the Policy Objectives Component.

Just a year earlier Wildavsky (1973) considered the proposition that if planning is everything then perhaps it's nothing. MSUA's policy formation/policy research effort, which was virtually unbounded in domain and range, could have benefitted by a narrowing of its "spectrum of activities".

11. I am less uncomfortable than I might otherwise be with the sample, however, courtesy, of a gift of six (6) boxes of materials from Mr. Doug Ryan, former Director-General, Development Branch, of the Coordination and Development Wing. As a Ministry "original", and a longstanding member of the Ministry's Executive, Mr. Ryan had assembled (and generously provided to me) a number of policy/policy research documents that supplemented my own holdings.

12. The politician-to-politician "advice" is deemed to be especially important; after all, if they won't heed the advice of one-of-their-own, whose advice will they heed?

13. The presentation by Andras was in early 1970, and just several months prior to his becoming the first Minister of State for Urban Affairs. Presumably Andras would take his own advice upon assuming office; on the evidence located, however, Andras' enthusiasm for UIA peaked during the preliminaries and waned upon being named Minister.

14. As suggested in fn. 25, once Andras succeeded in confirming the idea of a Ministry in the minds of Cabinet and caucus colleagues, he was then obliged to put together the institutional nuts-and-bolts. His waning enthusiasm for UIA was, perhaps, understandable.

15. That is my impression from having worked on several projects that were near and dear to the Minister's heart.

16. Anyone who thinks that "jobs, jobs, jobs" was a phrase coined by the Mulroney campaign of 1984 is hereby disabused; it was a theme of the MSUA work program in 1978 (and in work programs of other departments no doubt) as part of the run-up to the 1979 election, and likely has been around for decades.

17. The magnitude of the Secretary's task is indicaed by Wellar and Lavallee (1976), and in particular by the figures relating constituents, subject matter, and activities.

18. "Maturing" is used in a relative sense, and is intended to connote more direction and control of policy pursuits than had existed in the earlier years when the Ministry was trying to build a ship of state and float it at the same time.

19. For further discussion see Cameron (1974), French (1980), and Richardson (1972) in Appendix A.

20. By way of clarificatiion, the documents listed for 1976 were largely generated by MacNeill in conjunction with Habitat, or were the results of policy and policy research efforts instituted in 1974-75 and realized in 1976.

21. Teron's thoughts are contained in an article by Jim Robb, "Urban Affairs to quit $8 million La Salle home".*Ottawa Journal*, May 22, 1976.

22. In addition to materials produced by Lithwick as speeches and presentations for Ministers and Secretaries, and to which their names were attached, he made a most substantive contribution to Canada's urban literature in the 1968-1971 period: see, for example, Lithwick (1970), which was a massive undertaking and signal achievement by any measure, and Lithwick and Paquet (1968).

23. In fairness it is noted that neither Tellier nor Laframboise came to the Ministry with an urban policy or research background. Hence, it was not unreasonable that policy/research initiatives were not pursued on a gung-ho, pro-active basis. Indeed, given the Ministry's "all things to all people" enthusiasm of earlier years, perhaps it was fortunate that they had a dampening effect.

24. The "flip-overs" involved numerous organizational as well as subject matter changes within the Policy Analysis Wing, and changes in relationships between the Policy Analysis and Coordination wings.

25. Simply put, it was more by accident than by design for research outputs to be readily amenable and timely contributions to the policy formation process.

26. As Crowley (1982) notes, there were few policy and research personnel with government experience at the Ministry. I suggest that while experience in government may have helped researchers at MSUA accept doing "quick-and-dirty" work, it was not a necessary condition for conducting methodologically sound research. On the other hand, however, policy persons with no government experience were thoroughly mis-cast, and a source of double jeopardy; internal "searchings" for policy contexts and directions wasted time and energy, and turned off researchers and Coordination Wing staff. Further, external musings and "pop"?policy proposals caused some agencies to get their backs up, others to regard the Ministry as trying too hard, and still others

to dismiss it as a silly notion of the Trudeau government.

27. The unevenness in the development of the UIA references is understandable: the themes themselves were in varying stages of development as a function of their place in the informational activity, level of enquiry, and problem appreciation spectra.

28. For policy research documents with an explicit UIA presence see, for example: Cameron et al (1972); MSUA (1973a, 1973c, 1973d); Banz (1974), Greiner (1974), Stone and Siggner (1974), and Swain and Logan (1974); Carroll (1975), Edwards (1975), Fowlie (1975), Homenuck et al, (1975), Lambert (1975), Martin (1975); Michelson (1975), and Sunga and Duc (1975); Boothroyd (1976), Brice (1976), Burke and Ireland (1976), Duc and Sunga (1976), Jackson (1976), Ray (1976), and Wellar (1976); Chibuk (1977), MSUA (1977c, 1977d), Scorrar (1977), Wellar (1977), and Ulrich (1977); and MSUA (1987), and Wellar (1978).

29. For those who may think that MSUA should have done only "applied" research, where was one to look for the "basic" *urban* research upon which to base the applications? Also, see the SIDCUA section for an additional comment on "ivory towerism".

30. See Wellar and Lavallee (1976) for a discussion of the executive-research group relationship.

31. The one international report which comes readily to mind as having an explicit UIA reference is that of the OECD (1981). For a critique of the urban scene in the U.S. see JRS (1979).

32. It is noted and emphasized that what follows in this section is indicative rather than conclusive, and is based on impressions rather than on the findings of a methodologically designed study of ministry documents. Further, particulars as they relate to individuals or units within larger groups are of necessity blurred. Those qualifications notwithstanding, differences between the Ministry's promise and performance vis-a-vis policy/policy research with a UIA perspective was readily perceived during the document review.

33. Due to the lack of published reports, these observations are based on work program statements of the Directorates in the Urban Policy Analysis Branch: Settlement Patterns; Metropolitan Community Development; Non-Metropolitan Community Development; Urban Economy; Energy and Human Settlements; Urban Networks; and Urban Environment. Note: these differ from the titles adopted when the major Teron re-organization was approved by Treasury Board in 1976.

SIX MINUTES TO SIX MONTHS

C.I. Jackson

Consider the Ottawa urban transit system. For the last ten years it has been a model for cities of comparable size, that cannot justify expensive rapid transit. Yet, fifteen years ago, the system was quite ordinary. There was a bus network run by the Ottawa municipality and another across the river in Hull. The two did make token trips into each other's territory, but the twain did not meet in terms of a one-fare transfer system. Neither ventured far into the adjacent municipalities in its own province, or even into the low density suburbs of its own city. Not surprisingly, the journey to work in the Ottawa region was over-whelmingly car-oriented; even to the central area, on which transit services focussed, car travel had a 2:1 edge over transit.

That pattern changed dramatically during the 1970s, especially in 1974-75. The federal, provincial, regional and municipal levels of government cooperated in a carefully orchestrated series of actions that transformed traffic patterns and individual behaviour. The transit systems remained separate in Ontario and Quebec, but they became the responsibility of regional governments (Ottawa-Carleton and Out-aouais). New cross-river routes were established for the specific purpose of creating a transfer mechanism between the two systems. The provincial governments, especially in Ontario, recognized that subsi-dies to transit systems, for both capital and operations, could be less expensive and socially more beneficial than continued attempts to meet the road needs of car-driving commuters. A federal agency, the National Capital Commission, converted a major parkway into tidal flow at peak hours, with one of the highways reserved solely for buses. Finally, the federal government established charges for parking by its employees which meant that the cost of downtown monthly parking for government employees went up overnight from zero to $40. Hitherto, for many people it had been more expensive to ride the inconvenient and limited buses than to take their car; suddenly it was both cheaper and more convenient, as express buses appeared in the most unlikely suburban streets.

The change was almost instantaneous and became permanent. Total ridership for OC Transpo, for example, increased from 37.5 million in 1972 to almost 85.4 million in 1983. "More than 70% of all downtown peak hour work trips are made on transit". These improvements have been expensive but it is suggested that "the increase in the public subsidy to OC Transpo is about 45% of the cost of the automobile travel it has replaced."[1]

What is so striking about this transformation was that it was not dependent on technology. Buses and transfer systems have been around for a long time, and so has rush-hour traffic congestion. Nowadays, it is true, every bus stop in Ottawa is identified by an individual telephone number, through which a computer will tell you at any time when the next bus is due, but that is the high-tech icing on the cake. The transformation was the result of imagination and cooperation among several levels of government. MSUA was involved in the changes, but only to a very small extent; the main initiative was regional and (financially) provincial. Nevertheless, few things illustrate so clearly the revolution in thinking about cities and the urban environment which took place in Canada during the early 1970s.

In their 1974 study of the Ministries of State experiment, *Knowledge, Power and Public Policy* (some of us involved in the experiment felt at the time that "Rush to Judgement" might have been a more apt title), Peter Aucoin and Richard French accurately noted that the 1971 proclamations establishing both MSUA and the Ministry of State for Science and Technology (MOSST) each combined an "extraordinarily broad mandate with rather meagrely detailed policy, research and coordination functions." They also suggested that this combination was "to plague both ministries", which may have been true but was, as they themselves demonstrated, inherent in the experiment. The mandate could have been less broad, and the functions more specifically defined, but the result would not have been a ministry of state.

Policy, research and coordination, at any rate, were generally recognized to be the names of MSUA's game. In retrospect, another term than 'coordination' might have been less threatening to other departments and other levels of government, and also a more accurate description of that division's activities, which were essentially cooperative rather than coordinating.

Meanwhile, what was originally the Planning and Evaluation (P&E) and subsequently the Priorities and Planning Division was created in MSUA at an early stage to provide direct staff support to the Secretary of the Ministry and indirectly to the Minister himself. Such policy planning groups are essential (or at any rate ubiquitous) throughout Ottawa (Jackson, 1976); in MSUA, however, a more precise definition of the Division's role was required, since the entire Ministry could be regarded as existing to advise the Minister on policy matters. Put more bluntly, if Urban Affairs continually had to walk through minefields of jurisdictional and power-broking hazards, P&E had to begin such delicate footwork in MSUA itself: what was the characteristic that distinguished a task as ours rather than someone else's? There soon emerged, therefore, an informal motto for the Division: "six minutes to six months". At the short end of that range, P&E was used to provide a fast response to whatever was thrown at it by the Secretary or Minister—for example, a request for comments and queries on a document to be discussed in Cabinet committee the next day. Usually, it could take a rather longer view, often acting as the initiator ('midwife' was our preferred term) for some activity that might subsequently be taken over by some other group in or beyond the Ministry. Broadly speaking, however, if the time horizon was more than six months, all we could offer was prayer. The staff of the Division never exceeded about six people.

So much for structure and philosophy, both of which are essentially pragmatic anyway! What this meant in terms of actual work can be illustrated by recalling some of the specific problems in which P&E was involved. Inevitably these are the most memorable, but they were also fairly typical. Memorable, however, is appropriate in another sense: what follows is recalled after a dozen years or more, and my memory may well be unreliable on details.

(1) *The Second Toronto Airport*

Yes, Virginia, there is no second Toronto Airport (Mount Hope, Island and Buttonville do not count). However, this example serves as a reminder that MSUA's contribution to intergovernmental cooperation came through assisting the prevention of unnecessary or undesirable developments, as well as through more positive activities.

Ten or fifteen years later, with Mirabel's failure still a sore point, it is easy to forget that in the early 1970s, airport building was still in vogue. To be fair, part of the reason for Mirabel's failure—a recognition that landing rights at Toronto could no longer be withheld from foreign transoceanic airlines -was a factor arguing for increased capacity in southern Ontario. At the time, neither MSUA nor, probably, the Government of Ontario, was against a second airport for Toronto as a matter of principle. What did alarm us was that the federal Ministry of Transport (MOT), which had the primary responsibility for planning and construction, began with a firm conviction that the site for the second airport should be west of the metropolitan area. A specific site was never identified to my knowledge, but it was to be somewhere near the western end of Lake Ontario.

MSUA's strong intervention against such a location irritated those at MOT charged with airport planning (though senior management in that ministry was much more understanding). The airport planners had not defined the general location arbitrarily, but on the basis of expensive consultant surveys that had analyzed the demographic, geographic and economic patterns of southern Ontario. These surveys clearly showed that population and economic activity, and the consequent demand for air transport, was in the "Golden Horseshoe" around the western end of the lake; in MOT's eyes that was therefore where it made sense to locate the airport. MSUA, however, was aware that it was precisely because growth pressures were most evident in this area that the Ontario government was concerned to encourage more development to the east of Toronto. In MOT the second airport was a response to a perceived need; to MSUA the airport represented a powerful potential element in regional and growth strategy.

MSUA did play a quiet role in interpreting the Ontario Government's concerns to MOT, and in persuading the Ministry to consider an eastern site. But Urban Affairs' role was scarcely crucial; the Ontario government made its position very clear, to the point of threatening to withhold water and sewer facilities if the site (east or west) was not acceptable. An eastern site (near Pickering) was identified, and land assembly was begun, but it soon became apparent that expanding facilities at existing airports was more sensible than repeating the Mirabel experience. Nevertheless, the site selection process, especially in its early (east or west?) stages, was a nice example of the emergence of a broader urban vision at the federal level, and the opportunity to maintain a federal-provincial dialogue based on the issues. One the one hand a provincial government was attempting the unfamiliar and difficult task of managing physical growth, and was finding that some of the most crucial pieces in the game were in federal hands. From MOT's viewpoint, its attempt to fulfill its mandate to provide adequate and timely airport capacity seemed to be blocked for reasons that were difficult to understand and were largely irrelevant to the task as the airport planners perceived it. The traditional Canadian question—is the problem in federal or provincial jurisdiction?—had to be answered in terms of mutual understanding rather than the traditional Canadian compromise, and this required time and dialogue.

(2) *Dispersal of Federal Employment*

A broader vision in Ottawa of the urban impact of federal programs naturally took some time to develop, as was well demonstrated by the question of transferring federal employment away from Ottawa to other cities and other parts of the country. Such matters are always delicate, particularly since the patterns of life of large numbers of civil servants and their families are inevitably affected significantly by such transfers. This is true whether an individual is moved to the new location or has to find alternative employment in Ottawa. The department or section that is to be moved will almost always resist strongly. To be effective, therefore, such a policy must be clearly conceived and firmly implemented by the government.

By the early 1970s some dispersal had already taken place, including the transfer of the Canadian Mint to Winnipeg. However, enthusiasm for more extensive dispersal developed in the mid-1970s, to a large extent because it was government policy to have a more visible 'federal presence' across the country. From this viewpoint, it mattered little to the Treasury Board Secretariat (which chaired the interdepartmental committee that examined dispersal options) what groups went where, so long as enough people left Ottawa and went to enough different centres. To MSUA, however, such groups were as much instruments of urban policy as were new airports. To take an example (hypothetical but possible); moving much of the Geological Survey of Canada to Alberta could be justified on the general grounds that a large part of the Survey's work was focussed on the Rockies and other hard-rock formations. From the standpoint of Treasury Board Secretariat (and no doubt of the Survey's staff once they became reconciled to such a move), Calgary or Edmonton would be the obvious location. To us in MSUA, however, the growth of those cities in the early 1970s needed no further encouragement, and even the 'federal presence' factor would scarcely be noticed in their current size and rate of expansion. Why not Lethbridge, which the provincial government was keen to develop as an alternative growth pole to Edmonton and Calgary? The point that is being made here is not that Lethbridge would have been the right choice (it should also be reiterated that the example is hypothetical), but only that the Treasury Board Secretariat (TBS), like MOT, was at the outset understandably little concerned with overall urban policy and opportunities.

(3) *Vancouver and Nanaimo Waterfronts*

Canada is fortunate that so many of its major cities are at waterfront locations: St. John's Halifax, Montreal, Toronto, Hamilton and Vancouver are among the most obvious. Too often, however, that waterfront was pre-empted early for transport uses, and both physical and visual barriers have separated the citizens of these cities from the water. In many cases, the economic rationale for such single-purpose use is long gone. For example, the inner harbour of Montreal was made obsolete by the St. Lawrence Seaway (grain is now transshipped much lower down the estuary), by air travel which replaced ocean liners and by container ships which require far more wharfside space than finger piers can provide. Yet the old structures remained empty and derelict, and the cost of demolishing an array of tall concrete grain elevators is as formidable as the structures themselves.

Even in Vancouver, where the grain trade still flourished, it was an accident of history that required all the boxcar loads of praire grain to be brought right to the waterfront for sorting and consolidation, rather than being consolidated east of the Rockies and then moved by bulk flows through Roberts Bank or a similar outport. Other parts of the waterfront, especially close to downtown Vancouver, were becoming derelict, and represented in the early 1970s a wonderful opportunity for redevelopment for multiple uses in a dense urban population core. Understandably the National Harbours Board (NHB) which was not in the urban development business, did not see it that way. Equally understandably, other levels of government were not anxious to pay market prices for such land, even if the NHB had been willing to sell.

Once again, transport planners had a narrower perspective than

MSUA, and once again, MSUA's main contribution was to buy time for that perspective to be modified. It was, after all, seldom a matter of a clash between incompatible objectives of different departments and different levels of government. More often the task was to find a way in which the diverse opportunities and aspirations of urban Canada could be accommodated within the framework of departments and agencies that had each hitherto maintained (and been expected to maintain) a relatively narrow focus for their activities. It needs to be said also that time was also required for the municipal and provincial levels of government to adjust to the opportunity for intergovernmental cooperation and to develop realistic proposals for such waterfront revitalization. Gradually, in Vancouver as elsewhere, departments and administrations with limited operational responsibilities came to recognize the wider opportunities, and became enthusiastic about them, but the process took time to accomplish.

In a little more detail, over a period of 12 months or more in 1973-74, Cyril Rosenberg of MSUA's Co-ordination Wing ("our man for British Columbia") and I represented MSUA on the Burrard Inlet Steering Committee, an informal co-operative mechanism through which the City of Vancouver Planning Department and MSUA explored possible options for waterfront redevelopment between Stanley Park and Main Street. Absent from these meetings, and no doubt rather suspicious of them, were such key actors as the National Harbours Board, Vancouver Port Authority, CP Rail (and Marathon Realty, its real estate arm), not to mention the provincial government. By January 1974, the Committee's consultant, Dick Mann had developed five possible scenarios, mixing a variety of land uses in different proportions for five different hypothetical clients with very different priorities. The scenarios emphasized, in turn, recreation and conservation; real estate development; extension to the waterfront of adjacent communities; mixed activity; and tourism.

These proposals were publicized widely in Vancouver, and there seemed to be a strong preference for some blend of the "recreation and conservation" and "mixed activity" options. (This was not as illogical as it sounds, since each of Mann's options was essentially a variation in emphasis; even the real estate scenario retained a substantial amount of open space.) By mid-1974 Mann had developed a model representing such a blend and suddenly everyone was taking the whole thing very seriously. Such interest could easily be interpreted as opposition: the

Greater Vancouver Regional District belatedly argued against new commercial space along the waterfront; the Port Authority wanted the ferry terminal at Main Street rather than the foot of Granville; the Harbours Board began to wonder whether the whole area might not still be needed for port functions after all, and one or two people still seemed to cling to the notion of a Third Crossing of Burrard Inlet as a (federally-financed) solution to most of Vancouver's problems.

All this was healthy and by May 1974 it was time for MSUA to ease itself out. The joint federal-city study had helped to change people's perceptions about the waterfront; now it was for the city, the region, and provincial government and others to get on with the detailed planning and the working out of an actual program for redevelopment.

Vancouver waterfront was big-league stuff; Nanaimo provided a similar example in microcosm. One of the few planned urban layouts of 19th century Canada, the city's street pattern was designed to use the amphitheatre-shape of the site, so that a large proportion of the population looked down onto the harbour area. In the early 1970s, the Harbour Commissioners responded to an unusual opportunity for development with proposals to fill in most of the harbour in order to provide a large timber storage and wharfage site. This, naturally, did not please many of the residents, who preferred to look at water rather than timber and trucks, nor did it attract the planners of the Nanaimo Regional District. MSUA became involved because it was pointed out that the Harbour Commissioners, though local residents, were federally appointed. With some difficulty, the Commissioners were persuaded to carry out a comprehensive study of the harbour site, and of possible alternatives. This concluded that, on navigational as well as environmental and urban grounds, a site at the end of a nearby peninsula was feasible and preferred.

(4) *Federal Urban Land Policy*

Few problems in which MSUA was involved could be swiftly resolved; many of the problems were complex, subject to changes over time and were incapabale of permanent solution. An exception was the adoption of a new policy on the disposal of federal landholdings that became surplus to the requirements of the department concerned. This was an example of what has been termed a "good, fast crisis."

One Friday morning I was out of the office, participating in a series of exercises devised by the Public Service Commission in order to develop a profile of the typical senior executive.[2] Deep into an in-basket of assorted 'nasties', I was told by phone to stop trying to solve fictional problems and return to the real world.

For some years the Department of Public Workks (DPW) had recognized that its traditional role as supplier of federal government accommodation was a rather limited one, and that there ought to be other strings to the bow of its mandate. Land was becoming a matter of concern and expense, even in Canada, and DPW saw its role expanding from federal buildings to federal land, at least in urban areas. It had no ambitions, at least at this stage, to take over the National Parks or the Yukon and Northwest Territories. DPW had apparently discussed its ambitions with the Treasury Board Secretariat, which was not enthusiastic. (Being unenthusiastic is, of course, TBS's prerogative and normal operating style.) TBS had also apparently reminded DPW that Cabinet memoranda involving other government departments normally needed to be discussed in advance with the departments concerned, and preferably should carry the signatures of the departmental ministers, as well as DPW's own minister.

If this was indeed what happened, such a cunctative ploy deserves to be preserved in the textbooks of bureaucratic techniques, for it may be confidently asserted that as the number of Ottawa departments associated with a Cabinet memorandum increases arithmetically, the difficulty of getting all the ministerial signatures involved increases exponentially. DPW had been persuaded that at least a dozen departments were directly involved; after six months it had collected about half the required signatures. A general election then intervened and most of the ministers returned to new portfolios.

This had its humourous side, if not to DPW, but there was also a real problem to be solved. At that time, government policy required that any item of value no longer required by a department or agency should be disposed of for the highest price through the Crown Assets Disposal Corporation. One reason that this agency was little known outside the government telephone directory was because the proceeds of such sales did not benefit the individual department, but went to the Receiver-General of Canada. Departments therefore had every incentive to hang on to their assets, in the hope that they could ultimately find a use for them. However, the policy did apply to land, and we at MSUA were well aware that many parcels of urban land in federal ownership might command prices that would not necessarily lead to the best use of these sites from an overall urban standpoint. One of the most obvious examples was Downsview Airport in Toronto. Its value for aviation was small and diminishing; while it remained in the possession of the Department of National Defence (DND) it was largely 'wasted' in urban terms. Yet if DND should suddenly decide to release it for sale to the highest bidder, a unique urban opportunity for Toronto might have been lost.

The reason for my urgent summons was that, the previous day, some impatience had apparently been expressed at Cabinet level about the delay in coming forward with any new policy ideas on federal landholdings. MSUA's minister, probably to his own surprise, had been requested to bring forward such proposals the following week. If we were to meet the deadline, the necessary Cabinet memorandum had to be in the hands of the Privy Council Office by Tuesday.

Out of a hectic weekend there emerged a document that, as I recall, recommended that the federal government's landholdings, especially in urban areas, should not be disposed of without an adequate review of the best uses to which the land might be put in future. DPW was identified as the appropriate body to undertake such reviews and it was also encouraged to monitor the current uses of land by federal departments and agencies. The memorandum went to Cabinet committee over the signature of MSUA's minister alone; it was accepted practically as it stood. DPW, which had barely been consulted during the preparation of the memorandum, was grateful but bemused: after all its own efforts seemed to have gotten nowhere, why did MSUA's initiative succeed? The answer is merely that the time was right, and that MSUA was there with a realistic proposal at the time it was needed.

Those hostile to the Ministry may be inclined to say that these examples have been recalled at length simply because they represent rare instances where MSUA had any influence whatsoever. That is not my own belief; to me they are good examples of what our policy planning group in the Ministry did day in and day out during the five years that I was associated with it.

Certainly, however, it is difficult to credit the Ministry with specific acts or exercise of power. As Aucoin and French point out, repeatedly and somewhat remorselessly, ''the Minister of State's mandate does not include a central function, his operations do not involve the expenditure of funds or the distribution of service to the community, nor is his ministry responsible for administering programs for a particular clientele.'' He was not, in short, in charge of a line department. Few ministers, and not many civil servants, are content with such a role. MSUA's principal clientele was among the other departments in Ottawa, and among provincial governments and municipalities, not with large numbers of voting citizens. To the provinces and municipalities, MSUA originally represented an invasion of a preserve in which the federal government had no constitutional business. Subsequently (among many municipalities and some provinces) it was perceived and used increasingly as an ally: a place on the federal scene that had some understanding of the complexity of urban issues confronting provincial and municipal governments. Even within the federal bureaucracy, where MSUA's role so often seemed to be ''find out what Department X is doing in that city, and tell them to stop it'', the Ministry gradually came to be recognized as a place that was able to translate and explain provincial and other objections to federal actions or proposals, and so avoid confrontations based on misunderstandings and divergent objectives.

The temptation, in a volume of this kind, to trace the cause of death as well as to write the obituary of MSUA, is almost overwhelming. Superficially, it is easy to argue that the Ministry was destined to fail. Not merely did it suffer from the lack of clout inherent in a ministry of state, it was also in a subject area where it could expect to find few friends either at the provincial or municipal level or within the powerful program-oriented departments in Ottawa with which it frequently disagreed. Central (now Canada) Mortgage and Housing Corporation, for example, reported to Parliament through our Minister. Although in principle it was a crown corporation with a clear and limited mission, it had, in the absence of any other federal urban agency, come to regard itself as an appropriate source of advice on urban matters at the federal level. MSUA was the new kid on the block, and CMHC could hardly be expected to witness its birth with enthusiasm.

My own experience at MSUA leads me to believe that such factors may have deterred MSUA's Ministers more than those of us in the Ministry. So far as most of us were concerned, I believe that we did not see MSUA as a federal intrusion on provincial and municipal jurisdiction, but rather as a mechanism to ensure that the federal government became more sensitive and responsive to the needs of urban Canada than it had been in the past.

Canadians, after all, had become an urban society almost against their will; the national image has been of prairies and tundra, Maritime villages and Ontario concession lines, not cities. In Ottawa there were several departments, such as Manpower and Immigration, or National Health and Welfare, that were sensitive to the character of urban Canada and to its changing needs. Others, however, tended to see their mandates in physical rather than human terms: Energy, Mines and Resources; Environment; Transport; Public Works. Simply *because* Ottawa had few specific jurisdictional responsibilities towards urban areas, the federal government was less aware of urban problems and urban needs.

Such needs were particularly significant in the 1960s and 1970s. "In the post-war period . . . Canada . . . experienced a higher rate of urban growth than any other developed country. . . Between 1951 and 1966, . . . urban regions absorbed all of our total population increase of 6 million people." That growth had been managed very successfully; provincial governments had in particular been both adventurous and resolute in creating new forms of urban government (regional districts in British Columbia, regional municipalities in Ontario, urban communities in Quebec, etc.) that could respond to the changing morphology, needs and opportunities of the cities. What was needed in Ottawa was a better understanding of what provincial and municipal governments were trying to do, and of the impact (positive and negative) that federal actions could have on such urban strategies.

If this sounds dull and unrewarding, it was certainly nothing of the kind. In our small staff group, our tasks were determined by the in-basket or the telephone call, and the variety of tasks and problems was immense and exciting. One of the hazards of a ministry that has no specific programs to administer may be a tendency to take a timeless, detached view of the problems, in our case those of urban Canada. Like our colleagues in the Coordination Wing, we were concerned that this should not happen, even if the practical solution to most of our problems required time to enable objectives to be reconciled and communication to replace misunderstanding. I believe that Urban Affairs did make a difference and I am proud to have been associated with the Ministry.

NOTES

1. These quotations, and other data quoted above, are taken from sources kindly provided by John A. Bonsall, General Manager of the Ottawa-Carleton Regional Transit Commission (OC Transpo).

2. CAP—the Career Advancement Program—had been in existence for some time as a 'fast track' for the identification, training and promotion of individuals expected to reach the senior executive (then SX) category in the Public Service. After a while, those running the CAP course noticed that more of us were making it through to SX outside the program than from within it. With commendable objectivity, they decided that this might be partly because their image of an SX might not be what the system was looking for. Consequently, a number of SX-1s and SX-2s were invited to take part in a series of tests to establish a composite profile of the 'real' senior executive. For what it is worth, the tests seemed to suggest that I had a messier desk than any other SX, and that I was also willing to act with a minimum amount of information. These findings may help to explain why I left the public service.

3. Jackson, C.I., ''Policy Planning in the Government of Canada'', in J.T. Coppock and W.R.D. Sewell, *Spatial Dimensions of Public Policy*, Oxford: Pergamon Press, 1976, pp. 20-41.

SECTION FOUR

FUTURE NEED

RESEARCH BASED URBAN POLICY

LEN GERTLER

Since I left the Urban Affairs Ministry in the mid-summer of 1974, I have continued to have an association in one way or another with the subject of 'urban affairs'. Immediately following my departure and return to the groves of academe I got involved, in co-operation with Ron Crowley, in an effort to interpret the research that had been initiated by Urban Affairs and to relate that to a broader appreciation of the cities of Canada. That effort saw the light of day in the book, *Changing Canadian Cities: The Next Twenty-Five Years*, published by McClelland and Stewart in 1977.

In the same period I had something to do with the initiation of a graduate research project by Angus Schaffenburg, then a Planning Master's candidate at the University of Waterloo who in 1978 successfully defended a thesis on the topic, *The Development of Federal Urban Policy: A Case Study of MSUA, 1971-76*. Then in the Spring 1979, I published in the *Canadian Journal of Regional Science* a paper on "The Challenge of Public Policy Research", drawing heavily on the MSUA experience. Finally, I was Special Editor of the Spring 1982 issue of the same journal on the theme of "Public Policy—Urban and Regional Issues." It included insightful contributions by Ron Crowley, Audrey Doerr, Allan O'Brien and Barry Wellar.

On the basis of all this, I would not go so far as to lay claim to recognition as the poet laureate of the decline and fall of the Urban Affairs empire, but perhaps I may be allowed to enjoy the humble status of an assistant coroner. The important point is that my report, in a sense, has already been filed. It is on the record to be consulted as you please. So why continue to bother about "Research Based Urban Policy"?

The best answer I can give is a bit complicated; it has two dimensions.

The MSUA was an experiment in building a new kind of institution. It was an innovation for the purpose of developing policy and advising government with respect to a broad policy field cutting across several departmental jurisdictions, and in a way that was deliberately divorced from the distractions of program delivery. Furthermore, its central institutional concern: how to create and sustain an effective information and analytical base for public policy, remains unresolved. The issue is generic and the Urban Affairs case serves as an illustration of a broad dilemma of modern governance.

Thus we are not here, merely expressing a passion for history—to set the record straight, so to speak; nor, a perverse curiosity in institutional pathology. I start from the premise that what we are involved in is a search for an answer to one of the compelling riddles of modern government. From this perspective the concern of this commentary will not be on the merits of this or that particular initiative of Urban Affairs. Instead, it will be on what we can learn about the experience of the '70s which might lead us towards a more productive relationship between knowledge and public policy, between research and intervention in societal processes in a country like Canada.[1]

The Context

It is by now part of the conventional wisdom that the Urban Affairs policy Ministry emerged on the Ottawa scene along with the general thrust of the new Trudeau regime towards rational government. And certainly there can be no doubt concerning the claim to rationality in relation to that legendary base-line of modern Canadian politics: the era of Mackenzie King in which inadvertence in government processes was raised to a high art.[2]

The foundation of "the rational model" in the Ottawa of the seventies was the Cabinet Planning System. It featured a two-tier structure presided over by the Priorities and Planning Committee chaired by the Prime Minister, and specialized committees in broad policy areas such as Economic, Social, and External Affairs and Defense. It is not the place here to go into the intricate choreography of the annual processes of priority setting and resource allocation in which strategic overviews, the Fiscal Outlook, the "Lakes and Lodges" meetings, the Fiscal Framework and Throne and Budget speeches were the major political-administrative artifacts. Excellent expositions of these processes have been given in books by Audrey Doerr on *The*

Machinery of Government in Canada, and by G. Bruce Doern and Richard W. Phidd on *Canadian Public Policy*. What needs to be highlighted is the attention that was given to two overriding processes: policy development and co-ordination. The first indicated a political will towards attaining a more sophisticated information and knowledge base for *public policy*. For the record, I lean towards a pragmatic definition of that term: the amalgam of objectives, strategies and instruments (be they expenditure, taxation, regulation, investment and enterprise or exhortation) that are deployed to meet publicly expressed individual and collective aspirations. In the Ottawa of the early seventies "policy" was the buzz word that reverberated in the corridors of power.[3]

Co-ordination was seen as the hand-maiden of rational public policy. It expressed a determination that the policy ideas that filtered through the administrative pipeline to Cabinet and its Committees should be treated in an inter-related way lest, for example, the right hand of environmental protection be contradicted by the left hand of industrial pollution. To achieve a style of government animated by these transcending processes certain things had to happen. Central agencies like the Privy Council Office (PCO) and the Treasury Board which were in a position to lubricate the new Cabinet Planning System assumed a highly strategic role; most line departments established policy or planning units; and some new policy agencies in broad, cross-cutting fields were created; hence, Science and Technology, and Urban Affairs.

Interpretation of the Mandate

Again, for continuity in this tale I can suggest a number of works which document in vivid detail the play of forces that brought "Urban problems" to the top of the agenda in the Throne Speech of October 8, 1970, and then the subsequent formation in mid-1971 of the Ministry of State for Urban Affairs. The papers and volumes cited in my opening remarks may do for a start. In line with the synoptic judgement that I seek, I want to recall briefly the mandate and institutional design of MSUA, and then to move on to a proposition concerning the reasons for its decline.

The Ministry's mandate and institutional design must be understood as being inextricably interrelated. Metaphorically, the men and women at PCO and Justice were given an injunction to walk on eggs without cracking them. Accordingly, they came up with what seemed like an ingenious formula: an agency that could insinuate itself between the line departments and the central agencies—really a specialized extension with respect to urban matters of PCO itself; and an agency which would have as its anchor two unassailable federal functions: co-ordination of well-established federal activities in such fields as housing, transportation and public works which affect urban Canada, and policy advice on this federal urban connection. Then added on to these functions were two bold initiatives—and this is where the fear of cracked eggs comes in—which had potential for influencing the entire climate of urban policy and urban development in Canada, while respecting constitutional sensitivities, particularly the provincial juris-diction over municipalities. My reference is to co-operation and liaison with the other actors in the urban policy process: provincial and municipal government, and private organizations; and to research on urbanization. These two together had the potential for transforming the urban policy process by making inter-governmental consultation the hallmark of the urban sector, and through an open research program progessively increasing the volume and quality of information commonly available to governments, community and special interest groups.[4]

On the role and potential of Urban Affairs research, I stand by my words written in 1979.

I wish to establish the link between the research function and what I have called the 'touchstone' of the Ministry's mission: the capacity to turn inwards to the federal system and outwards at the same time. The inference I draw is that a research program embodying [these] principles [dialogue, flexibility, openness and substantial funding of external, independent studies] could go a long way to serving both "gods". While steadily building the capability to meet the in-house and policy co-ordination and development needs, the research program, in the way it would be both reported and used, would contribute substantially to creating the sought-for consultative climate. Every-one concerned would have a "piece of the action". And whenever the participants in the consultative process would assemble around a table to explore problems or strategies, they would appeal to a common information base drawn from investigations across the country, and would share the benefits of enhanced insight on basic issues. This is not to say that harmony would prevail. There would, of course, be controversies and conflicts, but those based on differences in research capability, and access to information would be minimized, although never eliminated.[5]

Other wrinkles of institutional design added to the novelty and challenge of the new Ministry. Those were the inclusion in the Minister's portfolio of two Crown corporations, Central (now Canada) Mortgage and Housing Corporation, and the National Capital Commission; and the appointment of the Minister to the Cabinet Committee on Social Development and The Treasury Board. Thus, the Minister was handed a blessing that was mixed—some of the spending power which is conventionally associated with Ministerial clout, and with it the hazard of being drawn too deeply *into* what might be politically high profile program concerns, and correspondingly *away* from the demanding role of innovator in both policy substance and process. At the same time, participation in key Cabinet Committees would enable the Minister to pursue both the prescribed policy and co-ordination roles—on broad issues in Social Development and with respect to large projects in Treasury Board. However, just to make life interesting and to remind the Minister of the mortality of things political, the new breed of agency was declared to be of "a temporary nature; of such a duration as to enable them to come to grips with the policy problems assigned to them."[6]

The Decline

Today, with the benefit of hindsight, we know that after a relatively brief heyday, the Urban Affairs Ministry had a turbulent and difficult history. A considerable part of its institutional life has fortunately been documented in some detail. Some of the major symptoms of stress and non-fulfillment of its mandate were the following. I have selected five:

1. The lack of official, Ministerial-level participation of the province of Quebec in the Second National Tri-Level Conference on Urban Affairs, October 22-23, 1973, Edmonton.[7]
2. The abortive outcome of the Tri-Level Task Force on Public Finance which was initiated at the 1973 Conference, and which reported three years later in a form: monumental indigestible statistics, and circumstance that produced no results whatever.[8]
3. The performance of the Senior Interdepartmental Committee on Urban Affairs which, established by Cabinet decision in July, 1973, to institutionalize high level co-ordination of urban-related policy and programs, did not in fact get off the ground; meetings were

infrequent and the prescribed reporting to Cabinet through the Urban Affairs Minister or a parallel Cabinet Committee never materialized.[9]

4. The fate of the Canadian Urban Demonstration Program which, in anticipation of UN Habitat '76 was established in March 1974 to stimulate innovative projects through a multi-sectoral fund of $100,000,000; but then was unceremoniously cancelled in April 1975. Commenting on this, Allan O'Brien, who had been deeply involved both as President of CFMM and an member of MSUA's committee on the Program, wrote—"This may well have been the point at which the ministry ceased to become "established" and began its downhill slide to oblivion."[10]

5. The gradual erosion and trivializing of policy research in Urban Affairs which moved from a focus on major themes starting in 1972 to a motley collection of unrelated studies, and finally in 1977 to the dropping of the term "research" from the nomenclature of the Ministry.[11]

Stressing the downside of the Urban Affairs experience, it is not my intention to downgrade its positive achievements. The Ministry, throughout most of its life, was the beneficiary of the dedication and strenuous effort of staff at all levels. Some of its work such as that on the Inner City and Urban Growth made in my view, an enduring contribution. I find myself in agreement with the judgement of Audrey Doerr:

The Ministry of State for Urban Affairs was an important catalyst in focusing on policy issues and designing a research agenda in the field. . . .It stimulated critical thinking and it provided a base of experience of the strengths and weaknesses of policy organizations. It provided some new perspectives on the relation between policy and policy-related research.[12]

In seconding the motion of these remarks, it is precisely the relationship between policy and policy-related research that I wish to hold in focus. While research as an intellectual and methodological activity can be identified as a distinct process, in a government agency with a policy mission it really is, conceptually, inseparable from the other statutory functions of policy evaluation and development, co-ordination and consultation. Since by design MSUA was excluded from program delivery and any budgetary control of urban-related expenditures, the only avenue left to the Ministry was the power of its ideas in the decision-making process. The ascribed functions of the Ministry must be seen as a continuum of ends-resources-means. Policy and Co-ordination are in this sense Research in action.

Given this perspective, the critical consideration is the relationship of MSUA to the decision-making process of the Federal Government. Regrettably, the weight of the evidence indicates that the Ministry's institutional niche was from the start precarious if not entirely untenable. Analysts like Ron Crowley and Audrey Doerr make the point that the clout of a horizontal policy sector straddling many agencies and programs (for 'urban affairs' the count was 27 and 117 in 1971) depends critically on its relationship to the Cabinet. Practically and symbolically that requires an acknowledged secretariat position between the line departments and a Cabinet Committee—much in the style of the second generation Ministries of State in the economic and social spheres. In the latter instance there is some circumstantial evidence to suggest that their demise at the hands of Mr. Turner, was based on too much rather than too little power, but that's another story! Since an independent policy advisory status was never attained, the Ministry was left in limbo, vulnerable to all the play of sometimes lethal bureaucratic games.[13]

Any interpretation of an issue as complex as the fate of a federal government ministry runs the risk of over-simplification. Accordingly, it is necessary to acknowledge briefly the impact of both an internal and contextual factor. Within the Ministry, it must be noted that its original internal design: separate units for Policy, Co-ordination, and Research may have inhibited the functional integration on which its effectiveness depended.[14] And outside the Ministry, we can now see, thanks to the insights of Richard French, that there was apparently an intensifying rivalry during the '70s among contending planning systems operating from three different centres, namely the Privy Council Office (PCO), Finance, and the Treasury Board.[15] The slight hesitancy in this assertion is due to the fact that the French diagnosis has been challenged, but not demolished in the pages of *Canadian Public Administration*.[16] What is not in dispute, however, is the perception that in the face of competing policy stances, for example, the fiscal/monetary fine tuning of Finance versus the strategic intervention of PCO, Cabinet was having serious difficulty in identifying and sticking to priorities. Meticulous evidence is brought forward to show that the idea of an "industrial strategy" pursued from 1970 to 1975 was a victim of this malaise.[17] So little wonder if on occasion Urban Affairs got lost in the shuffle.

A Disturbing Question

It is my hope that you do not find the explanations offered to this point excessively convincing, because the life and times of Urban Affairs still leaves us with a disturbing question. What I am referring to is the striking contrast between the luminous clarity of purpose expressed publicly by the "architects" of the Ministry, and the denouement that we have noted. In the Throne Speech of October 8, 1970 we find these words:

One of the greatest of the challenges to individuality comes from the increasing pressures of urban living . . . To solve the problems (of urban development) will require an increasing share of the nation's financial resources; not to solve them, to permit unmanaged growth, would result in an unacceptable drain of the nation's human resources. To foster co-ordination of the activities of all levels of government and to contribute to sound urban growth and development, the Government proposes the reorganization of its urban activities under the direction of a Minister of State for Urban Affairs and Housing. The Government seeks, by making rational its efforts in these fields, and through consultation with those most deeply concerned, to help Canadians reach and implement the decisions that will determine their urban future.[18]

This outlook was further amplified, and altered in one significant respect, when the Hon. Robert Andras, the first Urban Affairs Minister, tabled the draft Order-in-Council in the House of Commons on June 25, 1971. The interesting part of his speech is this:

The Ministry is purposely named the ministry of urban affairs, not urban affairs and housing, urban affairs and transport or urban affairs and land management; and it is so named because its policy mandate is unrestricted and as wide as possible, while its direct operational role is non-existant. The ministry's role will be coordinative as between federal policies and their departments. It will be supportive of all relevant federal programs and projects on behalf of comprehensive urban policy.[19]

The perplexing question that is raised is why in the face of these brave new words was the Urban Affairs idea implemented in a manner which seemed designed for failure? Do politicians willingly shoot themselves in the foot? One is led to the conjecture of either a lurid

Machiavellian conspiracy; or to the possibility that the powers-that-were had a dim appreciation of the role of a research-based policy agency and of what it takes to make it effective. The first option gains some support from Douglas Hartle, former Deputy Secretary (Planning) to the Treasury Board. Referring to the then Deputy Secretary (Plans) PCO, he wrote in the Spring, 1983: "I do not doubt that he was intent on wresting power from mandarins and ministers and gathering it to the prime minister and, by definition, to himself. His insistence on the creation of toothless ministries of state, such as MSUA, represented, I think, the decision model he had in mind at that time."[20]

Notwithstanding the stature of Professor Hartle, since he was a deeply involved protagonist in central agency encounters, I feel there is an obligation to reflect on, but also to temper his somewhat austere judgement. I am left with the other part of the conjecture, and to deal with that I think we must shift to a more conceptual level of discussion. This may be worth doing because the issues of governance raised by the Urban Affairs experience are still with us.

Research in Public Policy: Issues, Concepts and Conundrums

At this time I take it as axiomatic that the collapse of Urban Affairs in the late seventies has left a conspicuous policy vacuum in Canadian urban policy-making. It is now, after the fact, too easy to say that this does not matter because urban issues are no longer important to this country. There is room for skepticism. Indeed, the lack of an effective monitoring and analytical agency at the national level has obscured certain realities which we as a country will sooner or later have to confront. There may be a reckoning.

My own researches have shown a pronounced bias towards the situation which so alarmed the Federal Cabinet in 1971, namely the expansion of the big metropolitan areas. In 1971 there were seven above a population of half a million, accounting for 42% of the population of urban Canada; in 1976, the figure was 49%; and at the last census in 1981 those centres, expanded to nine, made up over 54%.[21] Another telling statistic relates to the population of rural areas. Within a general downward trend (declining from 27% to 24% of Canada's population between 1961 and 1981), the country has witnessed a dramatic expansion of urban-based population into the countryside, so that today over 82% of rural population is 'non-farm'—10% more than in 1971 and 20% more than in 1961.[22] Urban policy will increasingly have to give attention to those issues: economic, social, spatial and environmental, arising from the encounter of city and country. This is a phenomenon which will be further accentuated by the rise of information technology, which will significantly increase the proportion of our population who will be able to choose an exurban residence while maintaining contact with their offices via a computer terminal.[23] To these issues of growth and structural adjustment are added in these stressful times the distributional issues that focus in the cities: jobs, training, social services, recreation, housing and the inner city which must respond to increasing numbers of dependent households. In 1985, there is no lack of an agenda for research based urban policy.[24]

In the spirit of reconstructing the basis for a future Canadian urban policy initiative, I will now invoke a few fundamentals about the role and potential of policy research. Let me give you a very concise interpretation. For this, I call upon the insights of Amitai Etzioni, James S. Coleman, and Raymond Breton, who in the early innocent days of the Institute for Research on Public Policy wrote an illuminating little book called *The Canadian Condition* and of course, all of this is filtered through my own, sometimes traumatic experience as a policy researcher.[25]

The important point of departure is to distinguish policy research from what Corry and Bonneau have called ''frontier research'': curiosity-based empirical and analytical investigation through experimentation and/or observation which has the purpose of discovering new knowledge. Policy research, by contrast, is a reflective kind of inquiry that tries to make sense of what we know in the interest of effective organized action on society's problems. One can catalogue a large set of differences between policy and frontier research: secondary rather than primary data; more synthesis than analysis; problem— rather than discipline-oriented; interdisciplinarity to address complex issues in contrast with discipline-defined issues; an accessible rather than technical vocabluary; and greatly concerned with communication to policy-makers and their constituencies, instead of the coolly indifferent intramural preoccupations of experts talking to experts.

This distinction that I draw between academic and policy research was an active concern in the Urban Affairs Ministry. Crowley in his 1982 comments observed that "for those from academic backgrounds, research is often an end in itself, and it would not be unfair to conclude that research staff in the early years of the Ministry did see research as a pre-eminent goal."[26] My own reflective observations written in the final year of the Ministry were: "Policy as a distinct species of investigation does not have deep roots in our academic soil. And because that was so abundantly clear in the product that flowed back from the campuses to the Ministry, it served only to deepen the two solitudes of professor and politician. From the viewpoint of the man in Parliament, the professor roared like a lion and produced a mouse."[27] I am now pleased to report a glimmer of hope. In the spring of 1984, a mixed group of academics and practitioners at a *Workshop on Research in Public Administration* gave some thoughtful consideration to "the respective roles of political decision-makers, policy analysts and academic researchers around public policy issues."[28]

It is inherent in the concept of public policy research that it is closely related to government. This is not because non-government groups and organizations, be they the Institute of Urban Studies or the Canadian Labour Congress, have no interest in matters affecting the state of society like unemployment or environmental health; rather, it is because many of the issues are functionally and territorially broad in their impact and require the attention of the state. What is not, however, self-evident from the definition is why policy research may be important to the state; and why we still care about research based urban policy in relation to the Government of Canada.

On this question, I have turned to a recent work by two people whom I perceive to be sophisticated spokesmen of contemporary Political Science in Canada. They are G. Bruce Doern, Director of the Institute of Public Administration at Carleton University, and Richard W. Phidd, Associate Professor of Political Science, University of Guelph. Their book, *Canadian Public Policy*, is a highly literate effort, comprehensive, with many valuable insights, and it has the virtue of expressing a definite position on the public policy system as a key component of the Canadian political system.[29] But, I regret that I can find very little insight on the role of research in government.

Their guiding concept of public policy is, from my point-of-view, both the strength and limitation of their perspective. Ideas are the mainspring of the system. These, operating at three levels: ideologies, dominant ideas and objectives are expressed in, shape and give life to the structures and processes of government. The state deploys a variety of instruments—taxation, expenditure, regulation, public enterprise and exhortation—to attain its ends. At any given time, the policies that emerge are the product of a complex array of forces: dominant ideas like efficiency, individual liberty, equity and regional diversity, as well as paradigms like Keynesianism or monetarism, which are given concrete expression in party platforms and Parliament; executive-bureaucratic influences; the play of interest groups; and the information and knowledge available to the system.

The interpretation of the latter comes to the crux of the issue raised here. Knowledge that is pertinent is seen to come from both intellectual processes and social interaction. Democratic policy-making must have both hard and soft information: "official statistics, quantitative and scientific data", on the one hand; and on the other, various kinds of judgemental, political intelligence generated from "Ministers, their political staffs, the party caucus, party professionals, the media, individual citizens and opinion leaders." It is observed that "knowledge is not necessarily power . . . only one basis on which influence may be exercised."[30]

All of this, from my viewpoint, is beyond reproach—as far as it goes. What is to be noted, however, is that there is no place in this exposition for a policy research function. In keeping with the concept defined in this statement, reference is to a process which is dedicated to *linking* the worlds of processed knowledge and political intelligence, which is primarily integrative and interpretive in style, and is possessed of the importance of contributing to the quality and productivity of policy discourse through effective communication to the main actors in the public policy process. This function is conspicuously absent in the exposition of Canadian public policy. Indeed, what are called "policy analysis units" are given short shrift; few do "genuine research", whatever that means.[31]

Policy Research and Legitimation of the Modern State

To further clarify the thrust of these remarks, I will conclude with an appeal to a line of thinking called "critical theory" which is mainly identified with a Frankfurt professor of philosophy and sociology, Jurgen Habermas. This is of particular interest to this discussion because of the implications in that theory of the concept of "legitimation" of the modern state.[32] Several strands of the theory can be brought together in a synoptic overview, as follows:

Legitimacy refers to "a political order's worthiness to be recognized" and to exercise political power.

The modern western state: Capitalist, technologically advanced and with a democratic heritage, attains legitimacy in two forms: procedural and substantive.

Procedural legitimation is based on processes in which agreement is obtained and decisions made in circumstances which participants feel are free and equal and without domination.

Legitimation related to matters of substance derives from effective state interventions to overcome the "dysfunctional side-effects of the economic process."[33]

A "social welfare state-mass democracy" seeks legitimacy by policies and programs addressed to the major structural risks of "developed capitalist economies", namely the disruptions of the business cycle; external costs of private production like those of pollution abatement; and unequal income distribution. At the same time the state must support the requirements of a capitalist economy on which it is dependent.

"The complementary relationship between state and economy results in a goal conflict—especially in downward phases of the business cycle—conflict between a policy of stability" in favour of the private business sector, and "a policy of reform meant to compensate for the social costs of capitalist growth, which policy requires investments irrespective of the business situation and of profit considerations."[34]

The tension between the two goals constitutes the overall public policy challenge of the modern state; failure brings the risk of delegitimation.

In the conditions of the modern state, the development and use of information and knowledge, in a strategic way, is critical to both forms of legitimation.

In the hands of an astute leadership, research becomes the vehicle for transaction between scientific understanding and the self-understanding of social groups, between technical capability and social needs.

When that kind of communication takes place openly without intimidation, it conveys a powerful symbolic message that reinforces the status of government.

The same interplay of expertise and public insight fostered in a policy research process enhances the state's capacity to deal with the endemic problems of the economic system.

"The advisory bodies concerned with research policy give rise to a new type of interdisciplinary, future-oriented research, which ought to clarify the—social preconditions of technical progress in connection with the cultural and educational level of society as a whole."[35]

The cultivation of the connection between knowledge, democratic decision making and social action provides the basis for a constructive response to the overall public policy challenge facing the modern state.

Instead of the downward spiral of delegitimation, the way is open for "rationalization at the level of the institutional framework."[36]

"Public, unrestricted discussion, free from domination, of the suitability and desirability of action-orienting principles" and of ways to deploy scientific-technical capabilities—"such communication at all levels of political—decision-making processes is the only medium in which anything like 'rationalization' is possible."[37]

Rationalization "does not lead per se to the better functioning of social systems, but would furnish the members of society with the opportunity for further emancipation and progressive individuation. The growth of productive forces is not the same as the intention of the 'good life'. It can at best serve it."[38]

This is not the occasion to attempt a validation of critical theory in terms of the Canadian experience. I suggest that it is sufficiently compelling to be pursued heuristically in the spirit of "if the shoe fits wear it." Its special interest in relation to public policy is the light it throws upon the potential of policy research in modern government. The prospect is raised that we greatly demean and underrate the significance of policy research if we conceive it simply as another technical process, instead of a strategic variable in the public policy system that can make a critical difference to the quality of government. It may be no accident that since the death of Urban Affairs in 1979, the urban-related policies that have flowed from Ottawa have given us little cause for celebration.

NOTES

1. Len Gertler and Ron Crowley, *Changing Canadian Cities: the Next Twenty-Five Years* (Toronto: McClelland and Stewart, 1977)
   Angus Shaffenburg, *The Development of Federal Urban Policy: A Case Study of*

MSUA 1971-76 (Waterloo: Master's Thesis, University of Waterloo, 1978)

Len Gertler, "The Challenge of Public Policy Research," *The Canadian Journal of Regional Science*, Vol. II, No. 1, 1979.

Len Gertler, Special Editor, "Public Policy—Urban and Regional Issues", *The Canadian Journal of Regional Science*, Vol. V. No. 1, 1982.

2. G. Bruce Doern and Richard W. Phidd, *Canadian Public Policy*, (Toronto: Methuen, 1983), p. 189.

3. *Ibid.* Chapters 10, 11, 12.

Audrey D. Doerr, *The Machinery of Government in Canada* (Toronto: Methuen, 1981), Chapter 3.

4. Len Gertler, "Challenge", pp. 76-79, 83,84.

5. *Ibid.* p.80.

6. Schaffenburg, *Development*, p.47.

7. *Ibid]. p. 108.*   8. Allan O'Brien, *"The Ministry of State for Urban Affairs: A Municipal Perspective"*, The Canadian Journal of Regional Science, Volumme V, No. 1, 1982, p. 92.

9. Barry S. Wellar, "Urban Impact Assessment in Public Policy Processes: The Canadian Record, 1968-1982," *The Canadian Journal of Regional Science*, Volume V, No. 1, 1982, p. 49.

10, O'Brien, "Perspective", pp. 92, 93.

11. Gertler, "Challenge".

12. Audrey D. Doerr, "Organizing For Urban Policy: Some Comments on the Ministry of State for Urban Affairs," *The Canadian Journal of Regional Science*, Volume V, No. 1, 1982, p. 100.

13. *Ibid.* pp. 96-97.

R.W.Crowley, "The Design of Government Policy Agencies: Do We Learn from Experience?" *The Canadian Journal of Regional Science.* Volume V, No. 2, 1982, pp. 112,113.

14. Doerr, "Organizing", pp. 97-99.

15. Richard D. French, *How Ottawa Decides* (Toronto: James Lorimer & Company, Publishers, 1980)

16. Douglas G. Hartle, "An Open Letter to Richard Van Loon (with a copy to Richard French)", *Canadian Public Administration*, Vol. 26, No. 1, 1983.

17. French, *How Ottawa Decides*, Chapters 5 and 6.

18. Cited by Schaffenburg, *Development*, pp. 51, 52.

19. *Ibid.* p. 56.

20. Hartle, "Open Letter," p. 90.

21. Leonard O. Gertler, "The Changing Metropolis and the Blumenfeld Blues," *Environments*, Volume 16, No. 2, 1984, pp. 27-29.

22. *Ibid.* p. 29.

23. Len Gertler et al. *Technological Futures and Human Settlement* (Waterloo: Background Paper to CMHC, October 1984)

24. *Ibid.* pp. 30, 31.

25. Amitai Etzioni, "Toward a Theory of Societal Guidance", *American Journal of Sociology*, 73, 1967.

James S. Coleman, *Policy Research in the Social Sciences* (Morristown, N.J.: General Learning Press, 1972).

Raymond Breton, *The Canadian Condition*, A Guide to Research in Public Policy (Montreal: Institute of Research on Public Policy, 1977)

26. Crowley, "Design", p. 114.

27. Gertler, "Challenge", pp. 83, 84.

28. Audrey Doerr, "Research Workshop in Canadian Public Administration," *Canadian Public Administration*, Vol. 27, No. 1984.

29. G. Bruce Doern and Richard W. Phidd, *Canadian Public Policy* (Toronto: Methuen, 1983)

30. *Ibid.* pp. 327, 328.

31. *Ibid.* p. 344.

32. Jurgen Habermas, *Communication and the Evolution of Society* (Boston: Beacon Press, 1979), pp. 178-205

33. *Ibid.* p. 194

34. *Ibid.* p. 196.

35. Jurgen Habermas, *Toward a Rational Society* (Boston: Beacon Press, 1971), p. 73.

36. *Ibid.* p. 118.

37. *Ibid.* p. 119.

38. *Ibid.* p. 119.

THE MINISTRY OF STATE FOR URBAN AFFAIRS: THE FUTURE OF ITS PAST

H. Peter Oberlander

MSUA was a creature and creation of its time. It was a strategic, significant and successful experiment in public administration in Canada. It was *strategic* because it was launched within the larger context of radical changes in governmental structure and administrative procedure during the first phase of the Trudeau years 1968-72. It was *significant* because it challenged the conventional wisdom in public administration by advancing the concept of separating policies from programs and aggregating policy responsibilities in a single Ministry while leaving the programs with appropriate delivery agencies. It was *successful* because it met its original mandate as envisaged in the Speech from the Throne of October 8, 1970:

To foster coordination of the activities of all levels of government and contribute to sound urban growth and development, the Government proposes the re-organization of its urban activities under the direction of a Minister of State for Urban Affairs and Housing. The Government seeks, by making rational its efforts in these fields, and through consultation with those most directly concerned, to help Canadians reach and implement the decisions that will determine their urban future.

MSUA was a bold, courageous and sometimes exasperating experiment in launching the Ministry of State concept and applying it to the area of urban affairs in Canada. If it was strategic, significant, and successful, why was it abolished after eight years of existence? My concluding remarks will focus on that question.

MSUA was created under the exuberant, creative and innovative thrust of Pierre Trudeau's first administration and commanded the hearts and minds of many new-frontier politicians and administrators at a time when innovation and creation was the hallmark of Ottawa and heralded a new position on the political map if not an entirely new frontier. As Michael Pitfield has already suggested, the government had objectives it was trying to achieve, policies that would serve those objectives, and programs that expressed these policies. The Ministry of State concept separated program responsibilities from policy initiatives and presumed that policy development would be implemented successfully and could best be achieved by separating it from the day-to-day continuing routine program delivery and reserving unto it powers of co-ordination between individual programs for explicit policy goals. It was to be a policy Ministry and function as a sectoral central agency providing a function similar to PCO, but within a limited sector or segment of substantive policies and programs. One of the reasons for making urban affairs one of two Ministries of State (the other one was Ministry of State for Science and Technology) in 1970 was the large number of substantive urban programs being administered independently by almost every Federal department. One hundred and seventeen major programs were spread throughout 27 different departments. It was clear that this fragmented and diverse range of programs with varying urban impact and consequences was the result of individual departmental and separate administrative initiatives and deserved pulling together, perhaps even co-ordinating, under a single or at least related policy umbrella, thereby improving the effective program delivery, the expenditure of public funds, and above all achieving an agreed-upon urban future.

Everything about the Ministry of State was to be new, novel and innovative. Everything had new names, including the office of the Deputy Minister as Secretary, and the Ministry itself was created by an Order in Council, Gazetted on July 1, 1971, after a lengthy but amiable debate on a hot July evening in the House of Commons. The Proclamation, passed unanimously, stipulated that the Minister shall formulate and develop policies for implementation through measures within field of federal jurisdiction in respect of:

(a) the most appropriate means by which the Government of Canada may have a beneficial influence on the evolution of the process of urbanization in Canada;

(b) the integration of urban policy with other policies and programs of the Government of Canada; and

(c) the fostering of cooperative relationships in respect of urban affairs with the provinces and, through them, their municipalities, and with the public and with private organizations.

Its mandate, in simple terms, had three objectives:

(a) to put the Federal government's house in order;

(b) to develop a national research-based policy for urban issues for Canada;

(c) to develop co-operation with the Provinces on a variety of specific policies and program issues, bearing in mind the constitutional reality of Canada.

I arrived in Ottawa for preliminary talks as to the role and responsibilities of the Ministry, a week after the Speech from the Throne. Two weeks later, on October 20, 1970, Canada's stability and particularly its power to govern was severely tested. The October Crisis was upon us and both the Prime Minister and the Cabinet clearly had other priorities than the creation of a new, frail and fragile Ministry of State. The October Crisis derailed the timetable for the creation of the Ministry and for a variety of reasons, once the initiative was delayed or lost, it was hard to regain. More of that later.

While the Ministry technically was created only in July, 1971, during the first six months of that year, intensive and far-reaching discussions began to shape the nature and character of this new instrument of public administration. It was clear not only that the Ministry had an urgent policy role but also that it had to prepare itself quickly and decisively as a useful instrument for managing urban affairs federally in a country that assigned urbanization and its many faceted process essentially to the 10 Provinces.

The basic question during that first six months of the Ministry's existence was where to start on its assigned mandate—how and where to find the point of entry into the urban system and how to balance the strategic choices between evolving long-term policies and providing urgent operational advice on federal initiatives and interventions in various elements of the on-going urban programs. While born as a policy ministry, it was clear from the beginning that credibility and responsibility for the Ministry as an instrument of policy administration would depend on early and decisive success in advice to the Cabinet on current urgent and specific issues. Balancing between long-term policy development and providing fire-fighting advice is traditionally difficult and was complicated by the personalities of the four Ministers and their expectations. Robert Andras clearly provided the stimulus for the Ministry's concept and its creation; intellectually he made the most important and significant contribution to its initial operation and deserves considerable credit for its success. Ron Basford came to MSUA after an important but incomplete career at the Department of Consumer and Corporate Affairs. He saw MSUA more as an operational department than as a policy instrument and provided major leadership in asserting MSUA's mandate throughout the Federal structure and Provincial bureaucracy. Barney Danson was the most enthusiastic and urban-centred MSUA Minister. As a Member representing urban Toronto and Ontario generally, his creative skill and energies helped the Ministry maintain and accelerate its intitial momentum during political complexities and frustrations. Andre Ouellet, deeply rooted in Francophone Quebec, saw the Ministry's constitutionally ambivalent responses correctly, but ultimately had to accept its demise as a political reality.

Let me illustrate the rise and decline of the Ministry through a few examples as a policy initiator and as a program co-ordinator. These examples might indicate that MSUA was a success, but its very success sealed its demise.

Where should or could MSUA start in this process of policy making? Where can the Federal government be effective without provoking the Provinces? Can it put its own house in order and thereby decisively affect the process of urbanization across the Provinces? Where can we start in dealing with the urban issues that are clearly *of* the cities and leave the problems that are *in* the cities to the Provinces and their Municipalities? I have chosen three examples: the first is management of Federal Crown lands.

To everyone's surprise, including the Prime Minister and his Cabinet, the Federal government was and remains the single largest land owner in Canada, including within its major urban areas. Among the six largest cities, the Federal Crown, through 19 different agencies, owned 200,000 acres of land in 1971/72, often strategic in their location and invaluable as an economic asset. Not only was the magnitude of that property interest startling to the Cabinet, but even more amazing was the fact that there was no single place in Ottawa that could tell us where it was, for what Federal contract purpose it was owned or used, or what income or costs were involved in this substantial real estate. Further enquiry revealed conflicting and contradictory policies. For example, land that was no longer used by a given agency was transferred to the Crown Asset Corporation for disposal as surplus land, while other Federal agencies were buying on the open market comparable, and sometimes even the same, parcels of land. Some departments pursued the disposal route aggressively and saw it as a source of income outside normal Treasury Board and Parliamentary controls. For example, the Department of National Defence since 1968-69 had a fixed or frozen budget. In disposing of what DND considered surplus land, an excellent annual source of income generated funds that DND at that time urgently required. In summary the Federal Crown owned vast and important lands which MSUA judged to be strategic to its mandate and useful in managing urban objectives.

The initial Memorandum to Cabinet re Land Management articulated the strategic role of land as a resource, with optimum social use as location and discouraged viewing land as a commodity for sale and a source of public revenue. The objective was to influence and ultimately manage urbanization though provincial and local development plans; the approach was to establish Federal Crown land as a strategic instrument and create a management device through which Federal lands could achieve local urban plans and at the same time conserve Federal assets while reducing conflict and competition between departments for strategic sites. The Cabinet document, submitted by July 1971 and accepted by Cabinet with considerable enthusiasm, recommended the creation of an inventory for unified management and appropriate use of Crown lands. Land was to be managed not by departments but by a central agency, and once land was in the inventory it should never leave it again; it could be used and re-used, under public and private initiatives and only in exceptional circumstances sold.

Land was to be managed as a resource for effective urban purposes under a tripartite Departmental committee. The management responsibility for land was to be vested in the Treasury Board; conceptually land was a Federal resource like money and personnel, already under Treasury Board jurisdiction. The Department of Public Works was to create and maintain the land inventory and MSUA was to provide the policy advice on use and re-use. Initially several Provinces, and above all the municipalities, supported the land management process enthusiastically. Granville Island in Vancouver and Harbour Front in Toronto are two excellent examples of projects that resulted from that Federal policy. Areas in Montreal, Quebec and Halifax provide other examples. The management function of the inventory and maintaining the land in Federal Crown ownership has survived beyond the Ministry itself; it has been changed only recently when the present government decided to review the land inventory, again identifying surplus land, and advertise for sale, for the first time in 15 years, land in Canadian cities under normal market conditions.

The second example deals with amendments to the National Housing Act in 1973 and the resulting National Housing act of 1974, and the third example deals with the Railway Relocation Act of 1974, which provided an important entry on behalf of assisting and rationalizing local urban development through prevailing Federal jurisdiction in the transportation system of Canada.

The three examples have one common denominator: land and the Federal government's ability to act within its own jurisdiction with strong leverage. This position reflected Trudeau's belief that Canada was more than simply the sum of the ten provinces and the territories. The use of Federal lands within the framework of local urban plans and their vigorous development within the public domain has clearly been a success.

The National Housing Act amendments of '73 and '74 all strongly supported the social component of housing need and initiated opportunities for considerable municipal planning and development through NIP, RRAP, AHOP and eventually the Co-op housing movement. In this area Federal initiative has continued successfully till today. There was one dashed hope for large-scale influence in the network of settlements across Canada. The New Communities provisions of the NHA '74, while duly enacted, were never translated into effective programs, largely through the unwillingness of the Provinces to become involved in long-term and strategic settlement planning. The municipalities for their part were equally timid and interpreted the lack of interest by their Provinces as a signal to ignore the Federal helping hand. The Railway Relocation Act falls into the same category. It was an important and golden opportunity to reclaim strategic central city land through local initiative with Federal grants for comprehensive development. The Provinces were sceptical and effectively stymied any local interest, despite strong and sustained local demand in Regina, Winnipeg, Kamloops and elsewhere.

The three examples dealt with the Federal mandate within Federal jurisdiction. Let me recall one other element which related to the Ministry's mandate to consult with the Provinces and create a network of co-operation that MSUA was beginning to weave. The umbrella structure was to be a Tri-Level Consultation nationally, regionally and locally. MSUA organised two tri-level consultations—Toronto '72 and Edmonton '73—in the context of the growing commitment to Federal/ Provincial Conferences generally, except in MSUA's case we were committed to bringing the municipalities into the process. MSUA argued conclusively that unless the 4,000 municipalities were given a seat at the table, urban issues in Canada would remain the bargaining chips between Federal and Provincial politicians and administrators concerned with policy and program management, rather than with improving urban life where Canada lives and makes a living.

MSUA defined three consultative streams:

(1) The national Tri-Level Consultation between representatives of the Federal and Provincial governments and their Ministers to discuss *policies* dealing with major national issues of urbanization.

(2) Provincial/Regional Tri-Level Consultation between the Federal government and one or more Provinces and their Ministers discussing *programs* to deal with Provincial or Regional issues of urbanization.

(3) Local Tri-Level Consultation between the Federal government, Metropolitan areas or Regional administrations to discuss and resolve *projects* dealing with local issues of significant urban impact.

The first Tri-Level Consultation under Senator Goldenberg's puck-ish Chairmanship was followed by one in Edmonton a year later, in each case raising expectations among all participants which became increasingly difficult to meet. While we wanted high level consultation, the Provinces and their Ministers wanted bargaining sessions dealing with money and specific projects. In this sense the Provinces and local Tri-Level Consultation had more success and continued to be operative almost to the end of MSUA.

Let us attempt to draw a brief balance sheet between success and failure. On the success side:

(1) *Policy as Program*

Urban impact and the full consequences of Federal programs were pulled together gradually through a variety of internal and external co-ordinative devices. Separating policy from program and aggregating policy initiatives in a policy Ministry proved a success as long as there was the political will of Cabinet and its members to act jointly and in a mutually supportive way. The most explicit success was in the area of land Federally owned but planned and managed for locally articulated goals and objectives. This process lasted well beyond the Ministry's existence; unfortunately it is currently being dismantled.

(2) *An Urban Voice in Cabinet, Federal and Provincial*

The solving of urban problems suffered from two disabilites around the Federal cabinet table. No one spoke for the cities or their needs since constitutionally they are the responsibility of the Provinces. At the Provincial cabinet level urban issues are fragmented and compartmentalized between Ministers responsible for housing, infrastructure, transportation or land. An integrated, urban-centred policy process—recognizing that all aspects of the city interact because they are interdependent—is rarely, if ever, achieved.

MSUA as a sectoral central agency highlighted the desperate needs of Canada's cities and began to impress upon the Provinces their own need to articulate relevant urban policies and programs provincially. Many of the provinces responded to that initiative at least structurally and often substantively. Ontario in a variety of ways gave the urban issues a strong voice in a Ministry of Intergovernmental Affairs and its linkage with Ottawa. B.C. created a comparable Ministerial and Departmental focus, as did Alberta and Quebec. The most visible response came in Manitoba which still has a Ministry of Urban Affairs as distinct from the Department of Municipal Affairs. Most Provinces accepted the policy emphasis in dealing with their cities as an active and interdependent network.

(3) *Research-based Policies*

Perhaps the most important area of success was in the research started in the Ministry and through its substantial financial support beyond its boundaries. MSUA provided the essential research base for policy options and administrative strategies. It left behind a very respectable research product, but more importantly it created a human infrastructure of academics and professionals now spread throughout the Federal services and all levels of administration in Canada, who carry on the research orientation in dealing with urban issues. Perhaps its proudest achievement is the Alumni of MSUA, well represented by its senior members at the University of Winnipeg conference and reunion, 1986. There is no doubt that MSUA is a good example of the legacy of the years of Trudeau, who emphasized a rational and systematic basis for decision making; MSUA did demonstrate the possibility of public administration by objectives to achieve goals, albeit vaguely perceived, and all that within the fragile structure of federalism.

On the failure side:

(1) *Success defeats itself*

As MSUA began to assert its mandate and began to operate effectively, success itself threatened the Ministry's existence. As MSUA succeeded in pursuing its mandate in Ottawa, the establishment within the line departments felt threatened. It was inherent in MSUA's mandate that co-ordination meant bringing together diverse and disparate programs above and beyond the heads of executive agencies. As MSUA offered advice in the field of transportation and its impact on urbanization and regional development, eg: Toronto Airport II and Mirabel, the Ministry of Transport felt threatened and felt its advice undercut at Cabinet level. As MSUA began to argue for an integrated rational land management policy, land owning departments considered it interference and again felt threatened, eg: the Department of National Defense and the Department of Agriculture. As a policy Ministry, MSUA was mandated to co-ordinate line departments and their programs with the ten Provinces—a tall task indeed, and one that ran counter to Ottawa's client-dependent tradition and loyalties. Only an exceedingly determined central government political will could have prevented ultimate failure. Indeed as the Ministry succeeded in managing interdepartmental and interprovincial affairs, those who felt threatened began to mount a concerted offensive. The initial derailment due to the October Crisis was the beginning of the unraveling of the Cabinet's will to support interdepartmental co-ordination on behalf of urban affairs. MSUA was created as an indication of Ottawa's resolve to deal with urban issues nationally and to manage its own "urban" relations with the Provinces while recognising the essential constitutional dilemma. Only the strongest and most explicit political commitment by a unanimous cabinet could have sustained such a mandate.

(2) *Urban issues lose priority*

During the seventies, particularly toward the end, urban issues lost their position on the political agenda of governments generally. External political events, like the oil crisis, inflation, and environmental degradation, demanded a different political agenda. Urban issues generally lost their political appeal for governments and their advisors.

The Provinces, having been alerted to the increasingly strong Federal position in urban issues, perceived a dire threat in a Federal/municipal alliance on urban affairs and demanded their explicit and exclusive Constitutional jurisdiction and ultimately succeeded in undercutting MSUA. The Ministry was offered up upon the altar of Federal-Provincial relations. Its demise may have helped pave the way for some constitutional accommodation.

(3) *Policy or Program?*

On the failure side, there is one open question—is it possible to separate policies from programs? Is it possible to separate policy initiatives from program deliveries, or is the "power of the purse" and the allocation of program funds the only valid clout in the hands of policy departments and therefore must stay in the same political jurisdiction? Is it possible to aggregate policy initiatives and disperse program implementation? There is room for continuing analysis and continuing speculation. One intriguing heritage of MSUA was the interest shown by several other federally structured states in this experiment in public administration with urban affairs. The most significant parallel experiment occurred in Australia which based its own Department of Urban Affairs and Regional Development on MSUA's mandate. The Australian experiment collapsed even more quickly than MSUA; here remain a variety of other lessons for students of public administration of urban affairs within a Federal system.

In conclusion, there is no doubt that there are limits to Federal initiatives in urban affairs in a Federally structured country. With increasingly assertive Provincial governments in the tug of war between Ottawa and the Provincial capitals, the municipalities are the "innocent" bystanders and are severely affected. While MSUA attempted to build an equitable structure and system through which to resolve urban issues that affected Canada as a whole, the Provinces clearly refused to accept such a possibility. Urban affairs remained synonymous with municipal affairs and the municipalities remained wards of their respective provinces. There was no constructive accommodation during the seventies, and there is still no will to a Constitutional resolution. We were close to it in Victoria in the summer of 1972 where a Federal-Provincial accord alluded to the place of municipalities. A decade later the Constitution, by a supreme application of strength and political will, was patriated—but without changing the provincial/municipal dependency. The agendas of government have now changed, and the primary issues are jobs, inflation, interest rates and other economic priorities. All these issues have a clear impact on the cities and towns of this country and vice versa. The constitutional changes implied by the Meech Lake Accord in 1987 are likely to have additional impact. MSUA pioneered the analysis of interdependence of social, economic, environmental and political issues through its studies of urban settlements from coast to coast. MSUA was sacrificed on the altar of Federal/Provincial relations, to satisfy the almost irrational preoccupation with Canada's 19th century Constitutional allocation of powers spearheaded by Ontario, Alberta, Quebec and B.C. The issues that MSUA was established to deal with have not vanished. In fact they have increased, have become more complex and more intractable as Canada increasingly becomes a dense urban network. Consequently, someone, somewhere, and hopefully soon, will re-invent MSUA perhaps in a different garb, but as an essential instrument of public policy to deal with urbanization from coast to coast, as the underpinning of an industrially robust but highly fragmented economy.

REFERENCES

(Note: The following References and Appendices were contained in Barry Wellar's paper).

Documents produced by MSUA officials or under the auspices of MSUA are contained in Appendix A, while Appendix B lists documents produced by non-MSUA sources.)

Ackoff, Russell. 1953. *The Design of Social Research*. Chicago: The University of Chicago Press.

Cameron, David M. 1974. "Urban Policy", in G. Bruce Doern and V. Seymour Wilson (eds.). *(Issues in Canadian Public Policy*. Toronto: Macmillan, 228-252.

Cooke, Philip. 1983. *(Theories of Planning and Spatial Development*. London: Hutchinson.

Crowley, Ron. W. 1982. "The Design of Government Policy Agencies: Do We Learn from Experience" in Len Gertler (ed.). *The Canadian Journal of Regional Science*, (Special Issue on Public Policy—Urban and Regional Issues), 103-123.

Economic Council of Canada. 1967. *Fourth Annual Review*. Ottawa.

French, Richard D. 1980. *How Ottawa Decides*. Toronto: James Lorimer & Co.

Hellyer, Paul, 1969. *Report of the Task Force on Housing and Urban Development*. Ottawa: The Queen's Printer.

Helmer, Olaf and Nicholas Rescher. 1960. "On the Epistemology of the Inexact Sciences", *Rand Memorandum 353*. Santa Monica: The Rand Corporation.

Hemmens, George. (ed.). 1967. *Urban Development Models*. (Special Report 97) Washington: Highway Research Board.

JRS. 1979. "Toward a National urban Policy—Critical Review". *Journal of Regional Science. 67-129*.

Lithwick, N. Harvey. 1970. *Urban Canada: Problems and Prospects*. Ottawa: The Queen's Printer.

Lithwick, N. Harvey. 1972. "Urban Policy-Making: Shortcomings in Political Technology", *Canadian Public Administration*. 571-584.

Lithwick, N. Harvey. 1982. "Prospects for Planning: Coming to Grips with New Realities", in Barry S. Wellar (ed.). *Prospects for Planning: Coming to Grips with New Realities*. Ottawa: Canadian Institute of Planners. 3-8.

Lithwick, N. Harvey and Gilles Paquet. 1968. *Urban Studies: A Canadian Perspective*. Toronto: Methuen.

Mitroff, Ian and Murray Turoff. 1973. "The Whys Behind the Hows", *IEEE Spectrum*. (March), 62-71.

OECD. 1981. *Assessing the Urban Impacts of National Policies*. Paris: Urban Environment Directorate.

Richardson, Boyce. 1972. *The Future of Canadian Cities*. Toronto: New Press.

Steger, Wilbur A. and T.R. Lakshmanan. 1967. "Evaluation Methodologies: Some Aspects of Decision Requirements and Analytical Responses" in George Hemmens (ed.). *Urban Development Models*. Washington: Highway Research Board, 33-76.

Treasury Board of Canada. 1981. *Guide on the Program Evaluation Function*. Ottawa: Minister of Supply and Services Canada.

URISA. 1983. *Decision Support Systems for Policy and Management*. Papers from the Annual Conference of the Urban and Regional Information Systems Association. Bethesda, Maryland: URISA Secretariat.

Walizer, Michael and Paul Wienir. 1978. *Research Methods and Analysis: Searching for Relationships*. New York: Harper & Row.

Watson, George and Dickinson McGaw. 1980. *Statistical Inquiry*. New York: John Wiley & Sons.

Wellar, Barry. 1981. "Impact Assessment and Conflict Management: Confirming Analytical Approaches to Development Planning", in *Proceedings of the International Symposium on Conflict Management*. Kyoto, Japan: Department of Transportation Engineering, University of Kyoto, 80-103.

Wellar, Barry. 1982. "Urban Impact Assessment in Public Policy Processes: The Canadian Record, 1968-1972" in Len Gertler (ed.). *The Canadian Journal of Regional Science* (Special Issue on Public Policy—Urban and Regional Issues), 39-65.

Wellar, Barry. 1984a. "National Urban Policy in the Coming Decades: Structural and Functional Adjustment to Settlement Systems by Dirigisme, Accommodation or Laissez-Faire?" Presented at Second World Regional Science Congress, Netherlands Economic Institute, Erasmus University, Rotterdam, The Netherlands. Ottawa: Department of Geography, University of Ottawa.

Wellar, Barry. 1984b. "Information for Effective Decision-Making by Rural Public Authorities" in *Local Leadership and Rural Development: Implications for Research and Extension*. Washington: Extension Service and Economic Research Service. U.S. Department of Agriculture, 31-39.

Wellar, Barry. 1986. "The Need for and Nature of a Policy Context for Rural Planning in the Coming Decades". Prepared for a Special Edition of the *Journal of the American Planning Association* (forthcoming). Ottawa: Department of Geography, University of Ottawa.

Wildavsky, Aaron. 1973. "If Planning is Everything, Maybe It's Nothing". *Policy Sciences*. 4, 127-153.

APPENDIX A

Selected Urban Impact Assessment Readings Produced by MSUA Officials or Under the Auspices of MSUA

The following documents are those which I located that had an explicit UIA reference—to the economic, social or environmental significance of urban consequences flowing from policy or program initiatives, or lack thereof—and which I recommend for students of the urban impact assessment perspective.

The readings appear in chronological order. Due to the Ministry practice of not attaching names or offices to many of its documents, some mis-attributions may occur. In this regard, when in doubt I listed MSUA as the source. Unless otherwise noted, the documents were published by the Ministry.

1972

Adelman, Irma. 1972. "Future Urban Research Interests and Some Possibilities for Extending Process Modeling to Include Urban Social Processes". Seminar Transcript.

Cameron, David et al. 1972. "A Strategy for Urban Policy Development". (with Appendices).

Crowley, Ron. 1972. "The Effects of an Airport on Land Values". A.72.4 Working Paper.

Kaplan, Harold. 1972. "Controlling Urban Growth". B.72.20 Discussion Paper.

Swain, Harry. 1972. "Research for the Urban Future". B.72.13 Discussion Paper.

Ulrich, Martin. "Macro-Urban Program Impact Model: Environment, Context and Rationale". B.72.17 Discussion Paper.

138

1973

MSUA. 1973a. "Concept, Plan and Strategy. (Prepared under the direction of Peter Oberlander, Secretary).

MSUA. 1973b. "Montebello Papers". (Prepared under the direction of Len Gertler, Director General, Research Branch).

MSUA. 1973c. "MSUA Presentation to Treasury Board Officials, May 30th, 1973".

MSUA. 1973d. "Urban Canada: Yesterday, Today and Tomorrow".

Robert, Carlier, Lavoie Inc. 1973. "Comparative Empirical Study of the Effects of Growth Rates on Canadian Metropolitan Areas". C.73.1 External Research.

Schindeler, Fred. 1973. "Research Programme in Urban Government Systems".

Seni, Dan A. 1973. "Preliminary Considerations on a Framework for Policy Development".

1974

Banz, G. 1974. "The Public Urban Development Process". Draft Memorandum.

Danson, B. 1974. "Notes for Remarks to the Canadian Real Estate Association". (Halifax, September 20, 1974).

Greiner, Andrew. 1974. "Land Policy Status Report".

MSUA. 1974a. Federal Urban Objectives: National Urban Pattern and the Management of Growth. (Draft) Cabinet Document.

MSUA. 1974b. "MSUA: Federal Response to Urbanization". Working Paper.

Saumier, Andre and Barry Wellar. 1974. "Results Accruing from Information Systems in Urban and Regional Governments: Contexts, Identification and Measurement, Appreciation". B.74.27 Discussion Paper. Reprinted in *Resources and Results*, Papers from the Twelfth Annual Conference of the Urban and Regional Information Systems Association (1975), 377-391.

Stone, Leroy D. and Andrew Siggner. 1974. Demographic Research Priorities Related to the Field of Population Distribution Policy". B.74.6 Discussion Paper.

Wellman, Barry and Marilyn Whitaker. 1974. "High-Rise, Low-Rise: The Effects of High Density Living". B.74.29 Discussion Paper.

1975

Carroll, R.C. 1975. "Urban Impacts Analysis: Approaches".

Danson, Barney. Remarks or Notes for an Address to:

1975a.   Canadian Institute of Public Affairs, Toronto.
1975b.   Conference Board in Canada, Winnipeg.
1975c.   Media Club of Canada Biennial Conference, Vancouver.
1975d.   National Joint Conference of the American Society of Planning
            Officials and the Community Planning Association of Canada,
            Vancouver.
1975e.   Pacific Science Congress, Vancouver.
1975f.   Royal Commonwealth Society and the Human Ecology Coun-
            cil, London, England.
1975g.   United Nations Association in Canada, Ottawa.

Edwards, John. 1975. "Proposal for a Land Availability Planning Assistance
    Program". B.75.7 Discussion Paper.
Fowlie, John. 1975. "Metro Satellites Overview and Near-Term Action
    Plan". (CMHC/MSUA Interface Development Group).
Homenuck, Peter, James Morgenstern and Ronald Keeble. 1975. "An
    Analysis of Social and Psychological Effects of High Rise". B.75.9
    Discussion Paper.
Lambert, Victor. 1975. "Les terrains peripheriques de Mirabel dans le
    contexte regional montrealais".
MacNeill, James W. 1975. "MSUA: Federal Responses to Urbanization".
Martin, Larry G. "National Urban Land Policy: A Review and Recommen-
    dations". B.75.5 Discussion Paper.
Michelson, William and Kevin Garland. 1975. "Differential Role of Crowded
    Homes and Dense Residential Areas in the Incidence of Selected Symp-
    toms of Human Pathology". B.75.1 Discussion Paper.
MSUA. 1975. "(Draft) First SIDCUA Annual Review".
Sunga, Preetom and Gerald Duc. 1975. "MSUA and the Federal Govern-
    ment". A.75.1 Urban Paper.
Swain, Harry and M. Logan. 1975. Urban Systems: A Policy Perspective", in
    Environment and Planning. A. 7, 743-755.

1976

Boothroyd, Peter. 1976. "Forecasts of Canada's Urban Future".
Brice, Max. 1976. "First Report on An 'Urban' Evaluation Process". (Re:
    Joint DPW/MSUA Study).
Burke, Chris and P.S. Ireland. Holding the Line: A Strategy for Canadian
    Development. Urban Prospects.
Canadian National Committee for Habitat. 1976. Habitat and Canadians.
Duc, Gerald and Preetom Sunga. "Description of Selected Federal Urban-
    Federal Programs". B.76.3 Discussion Paper.
Jackson, C.I. 1976. Canadian Settlements: Perspectives. Urban Prospects.

MSUA. 1976a. *Annual Report, 1976-1977.*

MSUA. 1976b. *Human Settlements in Canada.*

MSUA. 1976c. SIDCUA Secretariat Preliminary Draft: MSUA Interdepartment Strategy, 1976ĩ1978''.

Rawson, Mary. 1976. *Ill Fares the Land.* Urban Prospects.

Ray, D. Michael. et al. 1976. *Canadian Urban Trends, National Perspective.* Vol. 1, Toronto: Copp Clark.

Wellar, Barry. (ed.). 1976. *Information Technology and Urban Governance.* Ottawa: Supply and Services Canada.

Wellar, Barry and Laval Lavallee. 1976. ''A Methodology for Selecting R&D Studies in a Policy-Oriented Organization''. B.76.1 Discussion Paper. Previously published in Computers, Local Government and Productivity, Papers of the Thirteenth Annual Conference of the Urban and Regional Information Systems Association (1975), I, 391-405.

1977

Chibuk, John. 1977. ''Urban Form and Energy: A Selected Review''. Working Paper.

MSUA. 1977a. ''Annual Report, 1977-1978''.

MSUA. 1977b. ''Action Programs: Land and Housing''.

MSUA. 1977c. ''Community Impact Methodology''.

MSUA. 1977d. *Habitat, The United Nations Conference on Human Settlements: Report of the Canadian Delegation.*

MSUA. 1977e. ''Regional Activities Quarterly Report''.

MSUA. 1977f. ''Small Community Development: Ways and Means to Government of Canada Action Programs''. Memorandum to Management.

Scorrar, Doug. 1977. ''The Federal Government Decentralization Program: A Community Assessment''.

Ulrich, Martin. 1977. ''Federal Government Approach to Its Urban and Settlement Responsibilities: The Teron Model''.

1978

MSUA. 1978. ''Land Use Policy in Canada: A National Profile''.

Wellar, Barry (ed.). 1978. *The Future of Small—and Medium-Sized Communities in the Prairie Region.* Ottawa: Supply and Services Canada.

APPENDIX B

Selected Urban Impact Assessment Readings from Non-MSUA Sources

The following documents were in print prior to or during the life of the Ministry, and contain an explicit or implicit UIA (or IA) reference. That is, the documents reference the significance (economic, social, environmental) of urban consequences. The materials are indicative of the state-of-the-art of UIA work outside the Ministry, and provide a basis for comparing the Ministry's UIA effort with that external to the agency.

Advisory Commission on Intergovernmental Relations. 1964. *Impact of Federal Urban Development Programs on Local Government Organization and Planning.* Washington: U.S. Government Printing Office.

_____.1965. *Metropolitan Social and Economic Disparities: Implications for Intergovernmental Relations in Central Cities and Suburbs.* Washington: U.S. Government Printing Office.

Aucoin, Peter and Richard French. 1974. *Knowledge, Power and Public Policy.* Ottawa: Science Council of Canada.

Burton, Richard and Harvey Garn. 1972. "The President's Report on National Growth 1972: A Critique and an Alternative Formulation". Washington: The Urban Institute.

Chevalier, Michel and Thomas Burns. 1978. *A Public Management Strategy for Development and Environment.* Ottawa: Supply and Services Canada.

Clark, Robert. 1976. "Program Evaluation and the Commissioning Entity", in *Policy Sciences*, 7, 11-16.

Galtung, Johan. 1978. *Toward Self-Reliance and Global Interdependence.* Ottawa: Supply and Services Canada.

Gertler, Len. 1978. "The Challenge of Public Policy Research". Waterloo: School of Urban and Regional Planning, University of Waterloo.

Hatry, Harry. 1967. "Criteria for Evaluation in Planning State and Local Programs", for the Committee on government Operations, U.S. Senate. Washington: U.S. Government Printing Office.

Hodge, Patricia and Philip Hauser. 1968. *The Challenge of America's Metropolitan Population Outlook—1960 to 1985.* Washington: U.S. Government Printing Office.

Lowry, Ira (ed.). 1968. *Recommendations for Research in Support of Federal Urban Programs.* Memorandum RM-5503-HUD. Santa Monica: The Rand Corporation.

National Commission on Urban Problems. 1968. *Building the American City.* Washington: U.S. Government Printing Office.

_____.1968. *Hearings.* Vols. 1,2,3,4,5. Washington: U.S. Government Printing Office.

OECD. 1971. *Report of the Study Group on Innovation in Urban Management.* Paris: Environment Directorate.

Real Estate Research Corporation. 1974. *The Costs of Sprawl: Detailed Cost Analysis*. Washington: U.S. Government Printing Office.

Schaenman, Philip and Thomas Muller. 1974. *Measuring Impacts of Land Development: An Initial Approach*. Washington: The Urban Institute.

Science Council of Canada. 1971. *Cities for Tomorrow: Some Applications of Science and Technology to Urban Devlopment*. Ottawa.

_____.1976. *Toward a Conserver Society: A Statement of Concern*. Ottawa.

Swain, Harry (ed.). *National Settlements Strategies East and West*. Laxenburg, Austria: International Institute for Applied Systems Analysis.

Swain, Harry and Ross MacKinnon (eds.). 1975. *Issues in the Management of Urban Systems*. Laxenburg, Austria: International Institute for Applied Systems Analysis.

United Nations. 1976. *Report of Habitat: United Nations Conference on Human Settlements*. New York.

U.S. Congress. 1967. *Hearings* of the Subcommittee on Urban Affairs of the Joint Economic Committee. Washington: U.S. Government Printing Office.

_____.1967. *Urban America: Goals and Problems*. Materials Compiled for the Subcommittee on Urban Affairs of the Joint Economic Committee. Washington: U.S. Government Printing Office.

U.S. Department of Health Education and Welfare. *A Strategy for a Livable Environment*. Washington: U.S. Government Printing Office

U. Department of Housing and Urban Development. 1978. *The President's national Urban Policy Report*. Washington: U.S. Government Printing Office.

U.S. Senate. 1967. *Federal Role in Urban Affairs*. Washington: U.S. Government Printing Office.

THE AUTHORS

Arthur L. Fallick   Research Associate and Publications editor, Centre for Human Settlements, The University of British Columbia.

Len O. Gertler   Director, School of Urban and Regional Planning, University of Waterloo. Former Director-General of Policy and Research Branch, MSUA.

Victor C. Goldbloom   President and Chief Executive Officer of the Canadian Council of Christians and Jews. Former Minister of the Environment and Municipal Affairs, Province of Quebec.

C. Ian Jackson   Executive Director of Sigma Xi, The Scientific Research Society. Former Director of Priorities and Planning, MSUA.

Desmond G. Newman   President of Cametoid Limited. Former President of the Canadian Federation of Mayors and Municipalities.

H. Peter Oberlander   Professor of Planning and Director of the Centre for Human Settlements, The University of British Columbia. Initial Secretary (Deputy Minister) of MSUA.

Michael Pitfield   Senate of Canada. Former Clerk of the Privy Council and Secretary to the Cabinet.

Andre Saumier   President and Chief Executive Officer, The Montreal Stock Exchange. Former Deputy Secretary to the Quebec Provincial Cabinet. Former Assistant Secretary, Coordination and Development Wing, MSUA.

Barry Wellar   Professor of Geography, University of Ottawa. Former Senior Member of Policy and Research Branch, MSUA.